Praise for the Author

M000039492

"Danny and his team bring a high level of insight, knowledge, and integrity to the online business world."
                    -GUY KAWASAKI, CHIEF EVANGELIST OF CANVA AND
                              AUTHOR OF *THE ART OF THE START 2.0*

"I've been consistently impressed with Danny; not just how smart he is, but also how giving he is with his expertise and generous spirit."
                    -BRIAN KURTZ, FOUNDER OF TITANS MARKETING LLC,
                                      FORMERLY OF BOARDROOM INC.

"Danny and his team are a model of professionalism and quality. Anyone who's serious about online marketing should be following what they're doing."
                    -MICHAEL PORT, THE NEW YORK TIMES BEST-SELLING AUTHOR
                                              OF *STEAL THE SHOW*

"Danny Iny and his organization are an utterly thorough and high-quality team of people delivering excellent products. I love sending people to Danny and team because I know they're in good hands and will come out the other end super smart and ready to tackle the world."
                    -CHRIS BROGAN, CEO OWNER MEDIA GROUP

"He's always full of energy, insight and passion for what people need to learn to truly be successful. I would not hesitate to recommend him or his company, based solely on his kindness, integrity and intensity."

-MITCH JOEL, AUTHOR OF *SIX PIXELS OF SEPARATION* AND *CTRL ALT DELETE*

"Danny Iny always provides solid content you can apply to grow your business. He's the real deal."

-RANDY GAGE, AUTHOR OF THE NEW YORK TIMES BESTSELLER, *RISKY IS THE NEW SAFE*

"Danny Iny is revolutionizing internet marketing, courses, and all other forms of online education. His enlightened approach to generating a sustainable model for ongoing income and impact is rivaled only by the level of integrity that is present in everything that he does."

-HAL ELROD, AUTHOR OF *THE MIRACLE MORNING*

"Danny Iny is a superhero, plain and simple. It's why I endorse his products to my people, without hesitation. His only burning desire is to help his sphere of influence build long term online business, that change lives and create freedom."

-ANDRE CHAPERON, CREATOR OF AUTORESPONDER MADNESS

"*Danny and his team have built something truly special in the online business world: a place that people can go to learn, grow, and work in partnership with a company that cares as much about their success as they do.*"
    -CLAY COLLINS, CO-FOUNDER OF LEADPAGES AND NOMICS

"*Danny Iny is one of the smartest minds in the online marketing space. The work he and the entire Mirasee team are doing is truly industry leading. Above all else, they genuinely care about delivering results for their clients and students, which is far too rare these days!*"
    -JOSH TURNER, FOUNDER OF LINKEDSELLING

"*When it comes to building your audience and designing online courses, Danny Iny is one of few experts I trust and personally follow—and someone I recommend all my customers follow as well.*"
    -RYAN LEVESQUE, AUTHOR OF ASK AND CHOOSE

"*Danny is one of the very few that care about his customers, stay ahead of the crowd, and produce results for himself, his clients, and his customers.*"
    -RYAN MORAN, FOUNDER OF CAPITALISM.COM

"*We've all heard the old adage about "teaching a man to fish." I love Danny's ethic does because he doesn't believe in doing things any other way. A fantastic teacher, a brilliant entrepreneur, and exactly the type of guy I'd love to have on my team (if I couldn't have him leading it).*"
    -SEAN PLATT, FOUNDER AND CEO OF STERLING & STONE

effortless

The Counter-Intuitive Business
Growth Formula for Coaches, Consultants,
Authors, Speakers, and Experts

Danny Iny

MIRASEE PRESS

5750 Avenue Notre Dame de Grace
Montreal, Quebec
H4A 1M4, Canada
www.mirasee.com

Copyright © 2020 by Danny Iny

All rights reserved. This book, or parts thereof, may not be reproduced
in any form without permission.

Paperback ISBN: 978-1-7347725-3-1
Hardback ISBN: 978-1-7347725-4-8
E-book ISBN: 978-1-7347725-5-5

1 3 5 7 9 10 8 6 4 2

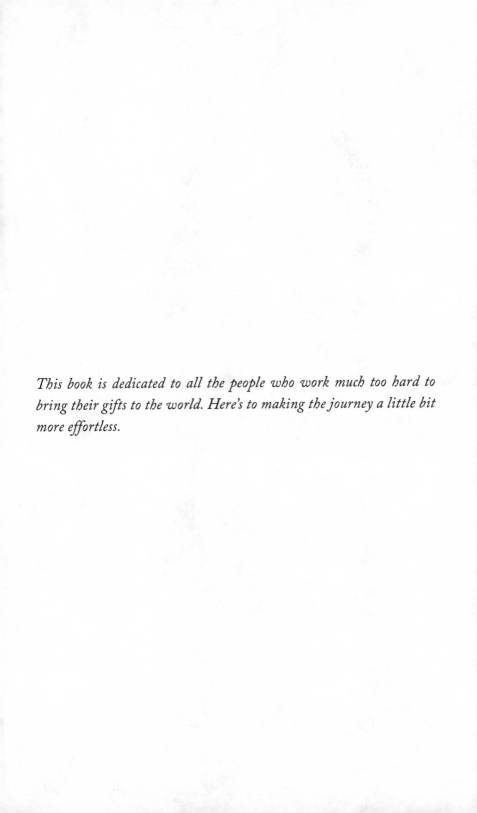

This book is dedicated to all the people who work much too hard to bring their gifts to the world. Here's to making the journey a little bit more effortless.

Download the AudioBook + Effortless Business Growth Toolkit (for FREE)!

READ THIS FIRST

Just to say thank you for reading my book, I'd love to share the audiobook version PLUS our accompanying Effortless Business Growth Toolkit, at no cost whatsoever—it's my gift to you.

—Danny Iny

Go to **www.Effortless.Rocks/toolkit** to get it!

Contents

The Midas Trap   i

    The Year of the Duck   iii

    From Futile to Effortless   v

    The Effortless Business Growth Model   vii

    How To vs. How Might I? (What Lies Ahead)   ix

Chapter 1: The Antidote To #Hustle   1

    Futile vs. Effortless   3

    Three Dimensions of Desire   5

    In the Eye of the Beholder   10

    Casting Your Ideal Customer Caricature   15

    Case Study: The Mirasee Ideal Customer   21

    Chapter Review   24

Chapter 2: Design Your Obvious Offer   27

    "I'm Sorry, We Can't Do That"   28

    Why You Can't Just Ask (Explicit vs. Implicit Desires)   31

    Evolving Toward a More Obvious Offer   37

    Case Study: The Obvious Business Acceleration Program   45

    Chapter Review   48

Chapter 3: Cultivate Your Resonant Identity   **51**

What Goes Without Saying   52

What Makes a Hero?   56
(Ingredients of Charismatic Leadership)

Resonance and Authenticity   64

Case Study: Why You Might Find Resonance with... Me   69

Chapter Review   72

Chapter 4: Lay Out Your Intuitive Path   **75**

The Path from Stranger to Sale   77

Escalating Cycles of Commitment and Reward   89

Case Study: The Path to LIFT   93

Chapter Review   98

Chapter 5: The Opposite of Futility   **103**

Effort Leading to Effortlessness   104

Never Finished   106

In the Agency of Others   111

About the Author   113

The Midas Trap

"A mistake that makes you humble is better than an achievement that makes you arrogant."

-UNKNOWN

STEVE JOBS was just 21 years old when he co-founded Apple Computer in his parents' garage, and just four years later it became a public company with a market capitalization of $1.2 billion. It's a vertigo-inducing ascent, but also a dangerous trap; the convergence of raw talent with the right time and place can lead to impressive results, but without the perspective that comes from experience, it can also create a cocky overconfidence—the feeling that you're a modern-day King Midas who can turn anything you touch to gold by sheer force of will. The next chapter of Jobs's story is well-known; product missteps and a tyrannical leadership style led to his ouster, and to Apple Computer's decline to the brink of bankruptcy.

Jobs is the most famous example of the challenging convergence of talent, opportunity, and inexperience—but hardly the only one. There are many such cases, and one of them is mine. The story begins back in 2011, when I was 27 years old; not as young as Jobs was when he started Apple, but still young enough that I had an awful lot to learn. I was driven and scrappy and had a knack for business and teaching, so I set up a blog and started writing. I liked experimenting with clever marketing ideas, and many of them seemed to work. The business took off, and I hit milestone after milestone in rapid succession: the $40,000 weekend, the $100,000 launch, the best-selling book, and million-dollar year. It was the stuff you'd hear from someone peddling a get-rich-quick scam—but this was real life! My solo consulting practice doubled in size every year through 2016, by which time I had a couple dozen people on staff, tens of thousands of people following my work, and a thriving customer base driving mid-seven figures in annual revenue. It was not quite the size or scale of Apple, but heady growth nonetheless.

January 2017 was going to see my biggest and cleverest initiative to date: The second edition of my book *Teach and Grow Rich* was coming out, to be followed by a major product launch. This was to be the launch to redefine what launches in my industry could look like—a much better experience for participants and a much more profitable endeavor for us. It was nearly a year in the making, a full-time effort for almost twenty people. I burned the ships and cashed in every favor; we were going to leave it all on the field. When all was said and done, we had over one hundred influencer partners on board, and dozens of content pieces that they could share. And it all came together beautifully. The book, which was free on Kindle for the duration of the launch, was downloaded tens of thousands of times. It hit #1 in the Entrepreneurship category, and #9 in the entire Kindle store (this was a pretty big deal; generally the top 100 books on Kindle are mostly popular fiction and celebrity memoirs). We were poised for the most glorious success in my company's history. And then, at the five-yard line, we fumbled the ball.

The Year of the Duck

In a split second of human error, well before the launch even began, the wrong box had been checked in our email marketing system. This meant that during the most critical window of our launch, 84% of our leads didn't receive a single invitation to enroll in our program. And then, our meticulous planning worked against us: Sales were still strong enough (from the small minority of leads who were given the opportunity to buy) that it took us too long to realize that there was a problem. By the time we found the issue, it was too late—the damage had been done, to the tune of almost a million lost dollars that I wasn't nearly successful enough to afford to lose.

That devastating blow was just the beginning. In the same way that Apple Computer's missteps in the early eighties were symptomatic of deeper issues of vision and leadership, the same was true for us; for the next couple of years we missed target after target, and bungled project after project. Our customers were happy and flourishing, but the business was floundering. So I buckled down and worked harder than I ever had before. I've come to call this time in my life the "Year of the Duck" because, like a duck, I had to appear calm above the surface, while under the water I was paddling as hard as I could! I knew the situation called for creativity and resourcefulness, and I rose to the occasion; I pulled a string of clever rabbits out of my proverbial hat, each time extending our runway of cash a few more months, allowing us to live and fight another day. But there are only so many rabbits that even the most resourceful entrepreneur can conjure. And those rabbits were of the "small win" variety—enough to keep us alive, but not enough to change the downward trajectory that we were on.

Those were dark days. My self-image as a brilliant and resourceful entrepreneur was under constant attack by the harsh light of reality, and I reassured myself that such challenges are just part of the journey to greatness—after all, doesn't every episode of Guy Raz's *How I Built This* podcast interviewing successful entrepreneurs include a story of being days away from insolvency? It's practically a required part of the formula, from the mighty Steve Jobs down to little old me! But in moments of honest reflection, I had to acknowledge that if I were wiser and humbler, I probably wouldn't have gotten myself into this mess in the first place. Finally, the urgency of the situation forced me to see it for what it was: things were getting harder and harder, and others in my industry were thriving—so where could the problem lie other than with me and the strategy that I had developed?

This was a turning point. I've since come to believe that an important part of maturing as an entrepreneur is developing a more honest (and sober) attribution of your success to the time, place, and circumstances upon which you apply your talents. Perhaps this is why many venture investors prefer to work with entrepreneurs who've had a serious failure in their history; it creates the space for bold and visionary instincts to be tempered with humility: No matter how bold your vision for the world as it could be is, you will eventually be confronted by the world as it is—and even Steve Jobs could distort reality only so far. But ego and arrogance aren't predestination; even Jobs could grow up, leading to the success of Pixar, followed by the modern array of iDevices, the iTunes Store, and the Apple that we know today as one of the greatest wealth creation machines in human history.

I grew up too. For me, that led to a question, which led to an answer, that put my business back on a trajectory of rapid growth—and to the book that you're reading right now. The question was simple: "Does it really have to be so hard?"

From Futile to Effortless

It came to me around the time that I was inhaling a series of business biographies, in hopes that the key of my salvation might be found in the story of a Steve Jobs, Elon Musk, Jeff Bezos, or Phil Knight. The question didn't come from any one of those stories but rather from the pattern that cut across them all. While these icons had moments of struggle to overcome, and they certainly worked as much as a person could, the growth itself didn't feel so hard. The bold strategies they developed and long hours they invested were paired with the ultimate force multiplier: customers that were excited about who they were and what they were selling.

When you really think about it, it's hard not to get hit in the face by the obviousness of it all. How could you possibly have rapid or exponential growth if it's an uphill battle to secure every sale? You can't, plain and simple. Steve Jobs's early success came from a brilliant insight that met the market exactly where it was, with exactly what it wanted. That doesn't take anything away from his talents or prescience about how important personal computing would be, but it's the alignment of that insight with what the market wanted that made it so successful—not Jobs's sheer reality-distorting brilliance. His product missteps all came down to a misalignment between what he thought the market *should* want, and what they actually did. People voted with their wallets, and in those days they cast their votes everywhere but Apple (and later, NeXT).

I had blundered in exactly the same way. My early success wasn't the result of a good idea alone, but rather a good idea that met the market where it was, with what it wanted. I was so focused on clever new ideas that I lost sight of the fact that, while those ideas were interesting and innovative, they were also increasingly out of alignment with what my customers wanted. It became increasingly clear that to change the trajectory I was on, I didn't need a fancy marketing strategy or innovative business model; I just needed to *give people what they wanted!*

Now, the advice to "give people what they want" is commonplace, but not particularly helpful unless you can also shed light on what it is that people in fact want. I needed a model for figuring that out, and I had a special vantage point from which to create one— the same model that I'm sharing with you here in this book. Sure, I knew the feeling when you aren't in perfect alignment with your market; every entrepreneur knows that feeling! But I also knew, from the early years, what it looks and feels like when you are. I knew what momentum feels like on a visceral level, and in reflecting on my experience, I could start picking out the key levers that had made the difference. I also had an ample sandbox with which to test and experiment: in addition to my own organization, I was working with thousands of other businesses through our programs, and got to see firsthand what worked, what didn't, and what circumstances seemed to tip the scales in the entrepreneur's favor.

The Effortless Business Growth Model

Three key levers emerged as I examined my own experiences and those of my students, crystallizing into a model for Effortless Business Growth—meaning that the more you pull on these levers, the easier growth becomes. Each lever is distinct and important in its own right, but they have a multiplicative, "greater-than-the-sum-of-its-parts" sort of quality, such that when you pull all three of them at the same time, the results are dramatic. Or at least, that's what I thought would happen. To borrow a phrase from Yogi Berra, in theory there's no difference between theory and practice, but in practice there is. Would this work as well as I thought it would, or would my team end up seeing this as yet another instance of the boy who cried turnaround?

Patient zero for this new protocol was my own business. Using the model, I pinpointed exactly where things had started going off course, and what needed to change. Then I set to work fixing what needed to be fixed, and surely (and not so slowly!), things started to get easier. The clarified focus was refreshing and energizing to us and to our audience. Sales ticked up, and we started hitting our targets. And of course, there's a virtuous cycle that kicks in pretty quickly; you execute on a good strategy, things go well, you feel better, and you have more resources and breathing room to work with, which make it easier to execute even better. In less than a year, the business completely turned around—both revenues and profits had grown dramatically, and our balance sheet was very much improved. Several members of my leadership team commented that they couldn't believe how quickly and drastically things had changed. It was like we were running a totally different company. We were still working hard, but it didn't *feel* hard anymore. It felt effortless.

I've since taught the same Effortless Business Growth model to hundreds of my students at my company Mirasee's intensive LIFT training event. They consistently find it both obvious and eye-opening, facilitating the sort of growth and ease that we all aspire to. These coaches, consultants, authors, speakers, and experts come from every continent on the planet, with expertise ranging from broad-appeal topics like painting, parenting, and human performance to specific and narrow niches like workplace safety, animal massage, and dream interpretation. Some of them are in the very early stages of "I've been thinking about starting this business and I'm ready to take the leap," and some are already running a thriving business, with a team behind them, and millions in annual revenue. Many are somewhere in between.

When business owners come to us, they often report feeling like they've been pushing a boulder up a hill. They don't mind hard work—in fact, they welcome it! But they're frustrated and disillusioned with the feeling of sheer futility, like nothing they're doing really matters, and that it's going to be hard forever. We help them to change all that by implementing the Effortless Business Growth model that you're learning about through this book, usually in less time than they expect it will take. Instead of struggling to make their marketing systems more effective, they tweak the structures so that it becomes effortless for their customers to want to buy what they're selling. And it works. Everything starts getting easier, and the momentum begins to build. It works so consistently well that when we support and train entrepreneurs in applying it, we're able to guarantee that they will earn back their full investments with us, and grow their businesses.

Now, of course a lot goes into delivering those results, from our team of world-class coaches to the systems and processes that we've built to keep our students on track toward success. But the ace in the hole, as it were, is the Effortless Business Growth model, which informs all the strategies that we develop. In this book, I'll share that model with you.

How To vs. How Might I? (What Lies Ahead)

My goal in this book is to share with you the Effortless Business Growth model—what it is, why it works, and how to apply it in your own business to achieve the growth you want, and to actually enjoy the process of making it happen. That said, everything I share won't boil down to a simple set of steps that you can mindlessly apply to grow your business. But of course, you already know that. You're smart enough to realize that the outcome of effortlessness in your business will take some effort to create!

That's why I encourage you to think of this book not as a set of "how-to" steps to follow, but rather as a "how might I?" invitation to wonder and explore. Use the ideas and models in this book to stretch your thinking, and ask yourself how you might apply them to your particular customer, offer, and business. Connecting these dots is a big part of the learning process and what will make it possible for you to come away from this book with new knowledge and a new skill set, which will serve you in good stead for years and decades to come. We'll explore these "how might I?" ideas though five main sections:

1. **THE ANTIDOTE TO #HUSTLE.** We'll start by defining what exactly we mean (and don't mean) by *effortless*, and then we'll introduce the model that you will use to achieve it. For good measure, you'll also learn how to quickly get to a place of clarity about who your ideal customer is so you can engineer your business around their wants and needs.

2. **DESIGN YOUR OBVIOUS OFFER.** Then we'll dive into the first lever of the model, which is the Obvious Offer. We'll explore what it means for people to love to buy, even as they hate being sold to, and you'll learn what it takes to turn your offer into the obvious choice for your prospects.

3. **CULTIVATE YOUR RESONANT IDENTITY.** The second lever of the model is the Resonant Identity. We'll explore the dynamic tension between its two component parts of Relatability and Aspiration, and the different ways in which you can convey both of them to your prospects.

4. **LAY OUT YOUR INTUITIVE PATH.** Next is the third lever of the model: the Intuitive Path. Here you'll learn how to craft the marketing messaging that communicates the things your prospects most need to hear so as to eliminate the friction standing in the way of their next step with you.

5. **THE OPPOSITE OF FUTILITY.** Finally, we'll close with an exploration of how to create systems of effortlessness in your business that create an ever-increasing momentum toward success. And, we'll discuss what you need to do when something unexpected happens and everything changes.

Along the way, I'll showcase how these principles apply to big businesses that you regularly hear about in the news, and also share behind-the-scenes examples from my own business. My hope is that by doing this, you'll understand the concepts more easily from the familiar and relatable business examples, and then go deeper with the sort of perspective that you can only have about a business when you're on the inside. I encourage you to study both the ideas and examples carefully. If you do so, you'll be dramatically better prepared to grow your own business. Effortlessly.

P.S. You do NOT need to read this entire book before also taking some next steps to connect with me and with my company Mirasee's business growth training. Feel free to take advantage of the invitations on the next page NOW.

Additional resources to support you!

GET THE AUDIOBOOK + EFFORTLESS BUSINESS GROWTH TOOLKIT

Get the free audiobook PLUS our Effortless Business Growth Toolkit, which contains valuable downloads and worksheets to help you apply these concepts to your business.

→ Download it at **Effortless.Rocks/toolkit**

ATTEND A FREE EFFORTLESS BUSINESS GROWTH WORKSHOP

Ready to lay out an Intuitive Path that leads to effortless growth in your business? Attend our free online workshop to go deeper into the ideas in this book and put them into practice.

→ Sign up for free at **Effortless.Rocks/workshop**

JOIN US IN PERSON AT LIFT

Discover cutting-edge strategies to accelerate your business growth through our immersive three-day training experience for coaches, consultants, authors, speakers, and expert entrepreneurs.

→ Reserve your spot at **Effortless.Rocks/lift**

CHAPTER 1
The Antidote To #Hustle

"Speed is irrelevant if you are going in the wrong direction."
—MAHATMA GANDHI

"DREAM HARD, WORK HARDER."

"The hard work puts you where the good luck can find you."

"Success is the product of hard work, persistence, late nights, rejections, sacrifices, discipline, criticism, doubts, failure, and risks."

"Dreams don't work unless you do."

It seems like hard work is all the rage in entrepreneurial culture these days. We fetishize it, as evidenced by a nearly unlimited number of sayings, quotes, and aphorisms proclaiming that if you want to succeed, you just have to work harder. The patron saint of the #Hustle movement is Gary Vaynerchuk, whose answer to the question of how many hours he works is "All of them!" And he has a point. Dig deep enough into any major success, and you tend to find that it was ten years in the making.

Consider Dorie Clark. She is one of the "Top 50 Business Thinkers in the World" (according to Thinkers50), the "#1 Communication Coach in the World" (according to Marshall Goldsmith), and "an expert at self-reinvention and helping others make changes in their lives" (according to the *New York Times*). Clark's success is born of the combination of massive talent and incredible work ethic, to the tune of hundreds (if not thousands) of articles in major publications, and four excellent books.

Or Mitch Joel. He co-founded the digital marketing agency Twist Image, grew it to become one of the largest boutique firms in Canada, sold it to advertising conglomerate WPP, and became president in Canada of the aggregated agency Mirum, leading over three thousand employees. In addition to all his work in the marketing world, he has delivered 40-60 keynote presentations for each of the last fifteen years, and his weekly podcast *Six Pixels of Separation* hasn't missed a beat since 2006.

The list goes on and the trend remains the same, whether it's Vaynerchuk, podcaster John Lee Dumas, or writer Jeff Goins (who all published daily content for years). It's even true for Mr. 4-Hour Workweek himself, Tim Ferriss. His ideas aren't the only reason he's the king of the business world: despite misrepresentations of his work to the contrary, Ferriss has one of the most extreme work ethics you'll ever find.

There is obvious merit to the idea that if you want to achieve success, you have to put in the time and reps to get there. And in an age where we expect instant gratification for no more effort than swiping right, we sometimes need reminders that hard work is both required and justified in pursuit of meaningful goals. So we put on the #Hustle-inspiring YouTube videos, crank the volume to full, and use the inspiration that it provides to kick-start us back into action. But for many, the inspiration is short-lived, simply because the "massive action" that they're taking doesn't seem to be creating any results.

Futile vs. Effortless

Greek mythology tells the story of Sisyphus, a self-aggrandizing and deceitful king. As punishment, the gods cursed him to spend eternity pushing a boulder up a hill, only for it to roll down every time it neared the top, which is why the most pointless and futile of tasks are described as Sisyphean.

Hearing the #Hustle stories of icons who've made it makes it hard to escape the feeling that the hard work they're describing is different in character from the Sisyphean labor that many entrepreneurs struggle through. Not that resistance and setbacks aren't a normal part of the process—of course they are!—but if you're on the right track, so is the feeling of traction. I'm sure that, especially in the early days, editors rejected many of Dorie Clark's articles, and other speakers delivered many of the keynotes that Mitch Joel had his eye on. But those setbacks were offset by the gigs that *did* work out. Gary Vaynerchuk tells the story of producing a *Wine Library TV* episode every weekday for nineteen months with only hundreds (and sometimes thousands) of people watching. That might not be enough to drive meaningful business results, but it's definitely a strong indicator that you're on the right track. Had his viewership held steady in single digits, he undoubtedly would have shifted his strategy. As Will Rogers put it, "If you find yourself in a hole, the first thing to do is to stop digging."

In fact, the most successful entrepreneurs I know see the process of building a business as a series of experiments in which you test to validate or disprove your hypotheses. Failed experiments are great, because they tell you what won't work so you can change course. This same approach is taught by the world's leading business thinkers, from Eric Ries (whose Lean Startup methodology preaches never-ending cycles of "build, measure, learn") to Jim Collins (who writes in *Great by Choice* that winning companies "fire bullets, then cannonballs").

The party line of #Hustle culture doesn't distinguish between the hard work of pushing a boulder up a hill and the hard work of rolling a snowball down one—but it should. Both take effort, but the feeling is completely different.

PUSHING A BOULDER UP A HILL IS FUTILE. No matter how hard you work, at the end of the day you'll be back to where you started. You'll be tired and sweaty, but also frustrated, demoralized, and hopeless. This is not the experience described by iconic entrepreneurs, unless they're telling the part of the story that comes before something shifted toward a better way of working.

ROLLING A SNOWBALL DOWN A HILL IS EFFORTLESS. That's not to say that it doesn't take time, or that you won't be tired and sweaty at the end of a day doing it. But the more you do, the more momentum builds, and the greater the payoff for your efforts. This is the energy of the success stories that we all crave and want to emulate.

This latter effortlessness is what entrepreneurs are hungry for—not the internet scams promising you will "make money while you sleep" so you can fulfill your lifelong dream of being a couch potato. On the contrary, entrepreneurs tend to be driven and energetic. We're more than happy to roll up our sleeves and take on big, exciting projects. We just want our efforts to bear fruit. What we don't want is to work tirelessly on something that will never go anywhere. We're desperate for someone to tap us on the shoulder, break our reverie, and show us a better way. The Effortless Business Growth model that you're learning in this book is that better way, and it works by satisfying the three key dimensions of customer desire.

Three Dimensions of Desire

My family and I have the good fortune of living in the Monkland Village neighborhood in the suburbs of Montreal. My wife and I first moved here as newlyweds, attracted to the boutique stores and restaurants, and proximity to the bustle of downtown. Now, almost a decade later, we have children aged five and three, and a very different perspective on what makes a neighborhood great. We still appreciate the restaurants and stores, but parks and schools are much higher on our list. And, of course, ice cream shops. Our neighborhood is rich with delicious ice cream options.

For years, we've had the big chain options: La Diperie and Yeh! Frozen Yogurt. And last year, a local mom opened Sandrini Confections, right around the corner from our house. So when my wife, the kids, and I want ice cream, where do we go? Our debates about ice cream choices are reminiscent of the debates that some readers will remember having with family or friends when visiting their neighborhood Blockbuster—each person has different criteria for what makes their choice the right one. All of those arguments, though, boil down to just three core dimensions of customer desire, and three corresponding levers of Effortless Business Growth: there's *what* customers want (and the Obvious Offer lever), there's *who* they want it from (and the Resonant Identity lever), and there's *how* they want to get it (and the Intuitive Path lever):

THE OBVIOUS OFFER (WHAT THEY WANT) – The first dimension is the desire to get the product or service that you want—the features and benefits, components and configurations, and price and payment options. The more closely you align your offer with whatever it is they want to buy, the more obvious your offer becomes.

THE RESONANT IDENTITY (WHO THEY WANT IT FROM) – The second dimension is the desire to buy from someone that they are eager and excited to do business with. This is about you, your brand, and the things that you stand for. The more you align identity with whatever it is that they care about and value, the more resonant your identity becomes.

THE INTUITIVE PATH (HOW THEY WANT TO GET IT) – The third dimension is the desire to buy in the time, place, and manner of your choosing. This is about the process of marketing and sales, and the steps that it takes your prospects through. The more you align the path to purchase with the steps they already want to take, the more intuitive your path becomes.

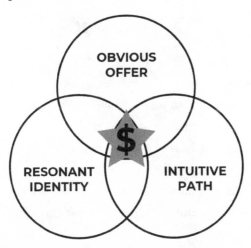

So how does that inform our ice cream debates? Well, the Obvious Offer to my wife and me is Sandrini (they have the best ice cream and the best vegan options), and La Diperie earns second place with their sugar-limiting mini-cones. My kids' first choice is La Diperie (for the toppings), and Yeh! isn't anyone's favorite. The Resonant Identity is also Sandrini (local entrepreneur with a sunny disposition). There's no obvious winner for Intuitive Path; Sandrini is right around the corner, but the lines can be a bit long, and seating space is limited. The other options are a longer walk to get to, and La Diperie usually has very long lines, but they do have comfortable seating. Yeh! also has good seating options and hardly ever has a line.

	La Diperie	Yeh! Frozen Yogurt	Sandrini
Obvious Offer	~	✗	✓
Resonant Identity	✗	✗	✓
Intuitive Path	~	~	~

So there's no clear winner, and we rotate between the options. But Sandrini has the most going for it, and if they ever got more seating or figured out how to shorten the lines, we'd never go anywhere else. But until they do, the rotations (and Blockbuster-esque debates) continue—because when it comes to the levers of Effortless Business Growth, two out of three just aren't enough.

WHAT ABOUT TWO OUT OF THREE?

When I teach the three levers of the Effortless Business Growth model, I sometimes get asked, "Which is the most important?" or "What if my business has two out of three?" The answer is that one is certainly better than none, and two will give you a strong advantage over competitors who have less... but really, this is an all-or-nothing sort of game. Because the combination of all three levers has a multiplicative effect, you really only reap the benefits when you get all three right:

- If you have an **Obvious Offer** and a **Resonant Identity** (but no Intuitive Path), you'll make sales easily, just so long as you happen to find yourself in front of the people you want to reach. But you can't count on that happening in a way that is predictable or reliable; you'll have the unfortunate distinction of being your industry's best-kept secret.

- If you have a **Resonant Identity** and an **Intuitive Path** (but no Obvious Offer), you'll build a horde of raving fans who absolutely love you, but don't actually buy anything from you. This is the predicament of audience leaders and YouTube celebrities who have millions of likes and followers, but still struggle to pay rent.

- And if you have an **Obvious Offer** and an **Intuitive Path** (but no Resonant Identity), you'll have a well-functioning funnel that does indeed bring in sales predictably and reliably, but you'll lose a lot of sales that could have gone your way, and find yourself competing on price and racing to the bottom. Think Lyft gaining market share because many people hate what Uber stands for.

There's no way around it: You need all three. In the following chapters, we will dive deep into each of the three levers of Effortless Business Growth, and you'll learn how to pull them in your business. But first, we need to know whose desires they are meant to satisfy; *obvious*, *resonant*, and *intuitive* are like beauty in that they exist only in the eye of the beholder.

In the Eye of the Beholder

The *Salvator Mundi* is an obscure painting thought to be a later work of the Renaissance artist Leonardo da Vinci. There is some controversy around its authenticity (not all experts agree that it was actually painted by Leonardo) and the numerous conservation and cleaning efforts that it underwent; somewhere along the way the difference between a replica and a highly restored original start to blur. Despite these questions, the painting was sold at auction on November 15, 2017, for the astronomical sum of $450.3 million.

The *Salvator Mundi*, sometimes attributed to Leonardo da Vinci

The auction price tag makes the *Salvator Mundi* the most expensive painting ever sold. But does that make it the best? Hardly—I think you'd be hard-pressed to even make the case that it's the best painting by Leonardo da Vinci! Consider, for example, the approachable beauty of his first version of *The Madonna of the Rocks*, the inspiring possibilities suggested by his *Vitruvian Man*, the mysterious smile of the *Mona Lisa*, or the piercing self-awareness of his *Turin Self-Portrait*.

Leonardo da Vinci's *Madonna of the Rocks, Vitruvian Man, Mona Lisa,* and *Turin Self-Portrait*

You could make a good argument for why any of these pieces is the best, but it's not a debate that can ever be won. Fundamentally, whether a painting is the best or most beautiful is true only in the eye of the beholder. In the same way, the obviousness of an offer, the resonance of an identity, and the intuitiveness of a path can only ever exist in relation to the needs and wants of a particular customer. Going back to the ice cream debates in my family, the decision will greatly depend on who's going; my kids care a lot more than I do about candy toppings, vegan options matter a lot more if my mom is joining us, and so on.

This isn't about having the "right" answer, the "best" marketing, or the "cleverest" funnel—because none of those things actually exist!

Effortless Business Growth is about aligning everything that you do with your ideal customer. The more closely aligned the offer, identity, and path are with the customer's desires, the more effortless your growth will become. Which means that, before we can talk about the levers of growth, we have to get crystal clear about in whose service they will be pulled. We need to identify our ideal customer.

WHEN CUSTOMER AVATARS GO BAD

A quick Google search for terms like "ideal customer," "customer profile," and "customer avatar" will yield more resources and information than you could review in a lifetime. And yet, despite the abundance of resources on the topic, entrepreneurs report that one of their greatest challenges is clearly identifying their ideal customer avatar, which is the stand-in persona that is held in mind when creating offers and marketing materials. It is also one of the most common things that marketing consultants have to fix when they get involved with a business, meaning that even businesses that think they're doing it right usually aren't.

The first mistake entrepreneurs make is selecting a customer avatar that is just way too broad. In an effort to keep the doors open to as many potential customers as possible, the net has been cast so wide that the avatar isn't specific enough for you to make any useful decisions about what your customers want, or how to reach them. If your customer avatar is "entrepreneurs," "women," "people who care about their health," or any other similarly vaguely defined group, it's too broad. Usually, this is a problem for people who haven't done the work to identify their ideal customer.

When that doesn't work, they seek out the advice of marketers, who advise them to choose a customer avatar that is narrow and specific ("the riches are in the niches!"). So entrepreneurs overcorrect, going from not enough detail to having way too much. They download customer avatar creation worksheets laden with questions about every facet of a hypothetical customer. And while they do their best to keep a real customer in mind when they answer the questions, there's a lot they just don't know about them. So what can they do but start making things up? Almost invariably, the result reads like a much-too-long online dating profile, so overloaded with information that it's hard to tell the relevant details from the red herrings.

What's the right amount of detail? Remember what these avatars are for: predicting what your customers will like (and dislike), and how they will behave. That's why the best customer avatars sit in the Goldilocks middle between too little detail and too much. They contain just the key details that allow you to call a clear *stereotype* of your customer to mind, and nothing more. And while the word *stereotype* often has negative connotations, in this case it is exactly the right word: The whole point is to call to mind something that represents a category (*type*) that encompasses many people (*stereo*). And while any individual is richer and more nuanced than the caricature that stereotypes might reduce them to, in this case the caricature is exactly what we want.

Imagine, for example, that a friend is setting you up on a blind date. You'll want some high-level information that you can mostly take for granted if your friend is introducing you—like their age, job, education, general level of attractiveness, and maybe whether they're a pet person. None of this tells you whether you'll like the actual person in question, but it does tell you whether they're in the *category* of people that you're looking to meet. Assuming they are, you'll want to know a few things that distinguish them from every other person in this category—like what kind of music or food or books or movies they like. So for example, a friend might say, "I want to fix you up with my friend Tina. She's thirty-one, really cute, and works at a big-five consulting firm. She's a foodie, kind of a hipster, and watches superhero movies to unwind." It's only twenty-four words of information, but really, what more do you need to decide whether this is a match you're interested in exploring?

Of course, this short description isn't a comprehensive representation of the multitudes that Tina contains. At this stage, that's just fine; you don't need all that to get a sense of whether or not she's someone you might want to meet. Later on, you'll want to know Tina the person. Right now Tina the caricature is not only acceptable, but also preferable. You don't want or need to hear Tina's life story to decide whether you're interested in a first date—not only because it's unnecessary, but also because even if your friend told you Tina's entire life story, you still wouldn't really know Tina. But you might have the *illusion* of knowing Tina, and that would all but guarantee that the date won't go well!

An overly detailed and disjointed customer avatar is like hearing Tina's entire life story before meeting her. As the image in your mind of who she is becomes ever more detailed, it will correspond to who she actually is less and less. And as a result, your ability to predict what she likes and how she will behave will be impaired, rather than supported. So for a customer avatar to be useful, we have to keep it firmly in the realm of caricature, where the mental picture of your ideal customer is simple enough to give you a clear gut sense about what they will like and how they will behave. To do that, we'll take a page from the people who do this better than anyone in the world: the writers of sitcoms.

Casting Your Ideal Customer Caricature

The first episode of *Friends* aired on September 22, 1994, and over the course of 235 episodes over the following decade, the world watched the exploits of Ross, Rachel, Chandler, Monica, Joey, and Phoebe. There's a lot that goes into making a hit show: an interesting premise, good writing, cultural relevance, and a healthy dose of good luck. A key ingredient, though, is a cast of easily understood and well-differentiated characters. Each of them is a caricature that is rich enough to feel like a distinct character, but simple enough for you to quickly and easily get your head around their desires and actions. That's why they can even serve as a sort of shorthand for describing others, and the same is true for any show that does a good job of creating well-differentiated caricatures for characters (which is why so much meaning can be conveyed by saying that someone is "such a [insert character from *Friends*/*That '70s Show*/*Frasier*/*Sex and the City*/*Desperate Housewives*/etc.]").

Chandler, Rachel, Ross, Monica, Joey, and Phoebe from *Friends*

To create this ideal customer caricature for your own business, start with the information that tells you the category of person that they fall into. In no particular order, here are the "big eight" demographic details that help you zoom in on a particular category of customer:

1. Gender (male/female/nonbinary/etc.)
2. Age (a narrow range like "early thirties" is okay, a broad range like 35–75 is not)
3. Family (married vs. single vs. widowed vs. divorced? kids, and if so, how many and how old?)
4. Geography (city vs. suburbs vs. rural? east vs. west? north vs. south?)
5. Income (do they work? what kind of job?)
6. Education (high school vs. undergrad vs. advanced degree? community college vs. Ivy League? arts vs. sciences?)
7. Politics (Democrat vs. Republican? and how strongly do they identify as such?)
8. Religion (faith and level of religiosity)

These should all be easy questions to answer, and they tell us a lot about the type of character we're talking about, but not enough to understand what makes them different from all the other characters like them. For that, we need to answer some specific questions. I'll share a list of questions that you can choose from, but the trick to doing this right is that you shouldn't make up answers to these questions. Rather, look through the list (or make up questions if you want to), for the short list of questions where the answer is so obvious that it just jumps out to you. In other words, if you have to think about what the answer to a question might be, it's not the right question for you to use; move on to the next one, until you have just five to ten with clear, obvious answers. Here's a list of questions to get you going:

- What books do they read?
- What's their favorite author or book?
- What movies do they watch?
- What's their favorite movie or who is their favorite actor?
- What music do they listen to?
- Do they have a favorite band?
- What kind of car do they drive?
- What kind of clothes do they wear?
- Where do they shop for clothes?
- What is their café of choice?
- What is their hot beverage of choice?
- Do they follow a particular diet (e.g., vegan, paleo, keto, etc.)?
- What is their cold beverage of choice?
- Do they fly business or economy?
- What's their dream vacation?
- Vegas or Broadway?
- Europe or Tahiti?
- DC or Marvel?
- Morning person or night owl?
- Apple or Android?
- Yoga in the park or boot camp at the gym?
- Paper or Kindle? (Or audiobook?)

Remember, the goal isn't to answer all of these questions, but rather to find the five to ten questions to which the answers for your ideal customer are super obvious to you. Armed with that instructive caricature of your ideal customer, we can now set to work addressing their core desires by pulling on the levers of Effortless Business Growth.

MULTIPLE CUSTOMERS VS. MULTIPLE STAKEHOLDERS

Some offers appeal to a single customer avatar—going back to the *Friends* analogy, Rachel likes designer handbags, Ross likes dinosaur museums, and Joey likes sandwiches. But there are also offers that appeal to all of the friends, like the Central Perk café. So what should Central Perk do—pick a single customer avatar to go after, or try to appeal to all of them? The answer depends on the relationship (or lack thereof) between those avatars.

If they're independent of each other (e.g., each of the *Friends* characters stops by Central Perk to get a to-go cup of coffee on their way to their respective jobs), then the café has the choice of whether to appeal to one, some, or all of the avatars. They might choose to focus on a single avatar. This is what I would recommend to most businesses that have that option, because every additional avatar has to be defined individually, which will likely add substantial complexity to the job of marketing, and may create a dynamic of contradictory forces that lead to pleasing no one in pursuit of pleasing everyone. In other words, if you have a choice in the matter, it's best to start with a single customer avatar, create Effortless Business Growth in your business around that avatar, and then add another down the line, if and when it makes sense to do so.

But they might not be independent of each other. Sometimes multiple customer avatars make decisions as a unit; the *Friends* characters are more committed to each other than any of them are to Central Perk, so they're going as a group, or not at all. In that case, we aren't talking about multiple customers as much as we are about multiple stakeholders: You need all of the parties on board for the purchase to happen, and each of the parties can essentially veto the deal. This dynamic is common when...

- Serving organizations (the end user and the payer may be different people, and they also need a sign-off from their VP of Whatever)
- Creating offers for children (since the child is the end user and the parent is the customer)
- Selling anything that costs much more than your customer can reasonably expect to spend on a weekly grocery run (that's usually the threshold above which a significant other expects to be consulted before a purchase is made)

In these cases, you need all the stakeholders on board, or you won't get any of them, so you have no choice but to create avatars for each, and do the difficult work of threading the needle with an Obvious Offer, Resonant Identity, and Intuitive Path that are aligned with all of them. In that case in particular, it is even more important to be hyper-focused and targeted about who your ideal customer is, because the broader the definition of who they are, the harder it will be to create alignment with their needs. This raises another question: What if you define the ideal customer too narrowly and miss out on great opportunities?

IT'S THE BULL'S-EYE, NOT THE BOARD

Before we wrap this chapter up, there's an important point to address that sometimes trips up entrepreneurs as they seek to identify their ideal customers. I'm talking about the risk of excluding perfectly good customers who don't fit the description. This fear is what often leads entrepreneurs and marketers to nudge their way into a broader (and less useful) customer avatar. To anyone grappling with that particular concern, I offer this comparison:

Imagine that you're holding a dart in your hand, taking aim at a board across the room. Your vision narrows to focus on the tiny red bull's-eye in the middle of the board, you lean slightly forward, and you make the most accurate shot you can muster. The dart hits the board with a thud, embedding itself two inches higher than the red bull's-eye, but squarely on the board. You didn't hit dead center, but it was still a good shot, worthy of celebration.

In this example, the red bull's-eye is your ideal customer avatar. You won't always hit it, and you can still celebrate the other customers who find their way to you. But you still need that precisely defined bull's-eye to aim for, because you can't hit a fuzzy target.

Case Study:
The Mirasee Ideal Customer

The gap between an explanation that we've read and an idea that we're trying to grasp can often be bridged with clear and specific examples, so I'll close each chapter with an illustration of how one company applied this concept: Specifically, I will illustrate with my own company, Mirasee. I've chosen to do this for a few reasons:

1. **INTIMATE KNOWLEDGE.** Whereas I can guess or infer at the strategies or decisions of other entrepreneurs and CEOs, I have much deeper knowledge of the company that I actually spent the last decade building, and spend my days running.

2. **CONSISTENCY ACROSS CHAPTERS.** Whereas I can find great third-party examples of Obvious Offers, Resonant Identities, and Intuitive Paths, it's more difficult to find examples that understand the model through and through, and have applied it in different areas.

3. **RESONANCE AND CLARITY.** This book is written primarily for coaches, consultants, speakers, authors, and experts—precisely the sort of person that my company serves every day. So presumably, our example will be relatable and relevant.

Of course, there are many other valuable illustrative examples, and they will be sprinkled throughout the chapters of this book (just as we have already touched on the examples of thought leaders, ice cream shops, renaissance artists, and television sitcoms). But to wrap up each chapter, I'll pull back the curtain and share our own thinking and strategizing around the people we serve, and how we serve them. Let's start now with our definition of who our ideal student is (we say *student* rather than *customer*, because we're an education company).

I've already told you that we serve coaches, consultants, speakers, authors, and experts—their role or profession is the thing about them that is top of mind, because it's why they need us in the first place (kind of like a restaurant saying that they serve hungry people, or people who like Italian food). Going a layer deeper, let's fill in the "big eight" demographic details. Our ideal student is:

- Female
- Mid-fifties
- Married with kids
- Living in a big city
- Upper-middle-class professional
- Well-educated, probably holding an advanced degree
- Politically liberal-leaning
- Spiritually inclined, regardless of religious affiliation

Now, remember the dartboard comparison; the person described above is the bright red bull's-eye, but that doesn't mean we don't serve lots of men and gender non-binary people, people who are both older and younger, people living in smaller towns and even off-grid, and so on—of course we do. But the majority of our students fit this description, because that is the avatar around which we've designed our Obvious Offer, Resonant Identity, and Intuitive Path.

Going a layer deeper, here are a handful of additional details to create a "flavor" of the sort of person they are:

- What books do they read? Social science and spirituality.
- What movies do they watch? Mix of popular films and documentaries.
- What kind of car do they drive? 2014 Prius.
- What is their hot beverage of choice? Tea.
- Europe or Tahiti? Europe, or maybe Latin America or India.

Hopefully, a picture is starting to take shape in your mind's eye. It probably doesn't describe you perfectly, because it doesn't describe any real person perfectly. This is an archetype. But if it feels resonant in the sense that you could feel comfortable in a group of people more or less like this, then that would be a good sign that you are our kind of person, and we are yours. Using this instructive caricature of our ideal customer, we continue our journey to craft the Obvious Offer, Resonant Identity, and Intuitive Path that combine to create Effortless Business Growth.

Chapter Review

Not all reading experiences are created equal. In the best of cases we're fully present and engaged, successfully soaking up every bit of detail and insight. But sometimes we read when tired, or distracted; noises in our environment might break our concentration, and thoughts within our minds keep our attention from fully fixating on whatever we're trying to read. The reading can become mindless, moving through an entire chapter without even realizing that you haven't internalized a thing for pages on end.

This is normal, and a problem that some authors address by simply repeating each big idea ten or fifteen times. I've opted for another solution: While endeavoring to be as concise as possible, I'll end each chapter with a quick bulleted review of the main ideas. I encourage you to read them as a sort of progress check for yourself. Ask yourself if you fully understand the point covered in each bullet. If you do, then you're all set, but if not, you might want to go back and revisit the chapter. Here is the first set:

- There is merit to the #Hustle culture idea that if you want to achieve success, you have to put in the time and reps to get there. Hard work is important.

- *Hard* and *Sisyphean* aren't the same thing. There's a big difference between the hard work of pushing a boulder up a hill and the hard work of rolling a snowball down one. That's the distinction between futility and effortlessness.

- Effortlessness is the result of alignment with your ideal customer on three dimensions of desire: the Obvious Offer, the Resonant Identity, and the Intuitive Path.

- The Obvious Offer (What They Want) is about the features and benefits, components and configurations, and price and payment options. The more closely you align your offer with whatever it is that customers want to buy, the more obvious your offer becomes.

- The Resonant Identity (Who They Want It From) is about you, your brand, and the things that you stand for. The more you align your identity with whatever it is that your customers care about and value, the more resonant your identity becomes.

- The Intuitive Path (How They Want to Get It) is about the process of marketing and sales, and the steps that it takes your prospects through. The more you align the path to purchase with the steps they already want to take, the more intuitive your path becomes.

- You need to be aligned with your ideal customer on all three dimensions of desire; two out of three will lead to easy but sporadic sales (Obvious Offer + Resonant Identity), lots of raving fans but no money (Resonant Identity + Intuitive Path), or a commoditized race to the bottom (Obvious Offer + Intuitive Path).

- There is no objectively "good" offer, identity, or path—just offers, identities, and paths that are obvious, resonant, and intuitive to a specific ideal customer. That's why identifying your ideal customer avatar is so important.

- Customer avatars should have a Goldilocks amount of detail: enough to know who they are and what they will respond to, but not so much that you are overloaded in detail.

- Identify your ideal customer avatar by starting with the "big eight" demographic details, and then filling in five to ten more things about them that are more specific to their character.

- It's best to start with a single ideal customer, as having more than one will double or triple the amount of work to do as you build your business, and create a lot of potential complications.

- But if you're dealing with multiple stakeholders, you don't have a choice; you have to make sure your business is obvious, resonant, and intuitive to all of them.

- Finally, remember that your ideal customer avatar is a bull's-eye, not a straitjacket—meant to guide your decisions, not constrain you from working with people who are eager for your product or service.

CHAPTER 2

Design Your Obvious Offer

"People don't like being sold, but they love to buy."
—JEFFREY GITOMER

THERE ARE FEW COMPANIES whose stories of success are as dizzying as Amazon's. Their staggering market capitalization (hovering around $1.5 *trillion* at the time of this writing) is the result of many bold moves, including the subscription model of Amazon Prime, the development of the Kindle and its e-book marketplace, the productization of their infrastructure as Amazon Web Services, the Amazon Marketplace (and the Fulfilled by Amazon infrastructure that powers it), and most recently the rollout of the Alexa smart speaker (and screen) systems. Entire volumes can and have been written about the strategy behind Amazon's ascent, but at the core it's very simple. In Bezos's own words:

> You can build a business strategy around the things that are stable in time. ... [I]n our retail business, we know that

customers want low prices, and I know that's going to be true 10 years from now. They want fast delivery; they want vast selection. It's impossible to imagine a future 10 years from now where a customer comes up and says, 'Jeff I love Amazon; I just wish the prices were a little higher,' [or] 'I love Amazon; I just wish you'd deliver a little more slowly.' Impossible. And so the effort we put into those things, spinning those things up, we know the energy we put into it today will still be paying off dividends for our customers 10 years from now. When you have something that you know is true, even over the long term, you can afford to put a lot of energy into it.

Low prices. Vast Selection. Fast delivery. This is Amazon's formula for an Obvious Offer. Your formula will probably be different, but the logic behind it is the same: figure out exactly what it is that your customers want, and then do everything you can to avoid the six words that they don't want to hear.

"I'm Sorry, We Can't Do That"

Sales guru Jeffrey Gitomer is known for saying that people hate being sold, but love to buy. The quote sticks in your mind because it draws a contrast between these two experiences that are often conflated, despite being worlds apart. Buying, in its purest form, is about seeing something you want and claiming it as your own. Buying is typified by the famous words of Julius Caesar, "Veni, vidi, vici"—I came, I saw something I wanted, and I made it mine. It is an empowering experience; no wonder retail therapy is such a popular pastime!

Being sold, on the other hand, is fundamentally an experience of being manipulated into compromise, and it only happens when you have misgivings about making a purchase. The words may never be spoken out loud, but we feel that we're being sold when an exchange goes something like this:

Prospect: "Here's exactly what I want."

Seller: "I'm sorry, we can't do that. But let me convince you that what I've got is fine."

I'm sorry, we can't do that. These are the six words that separate the exhilarating experience of buying from the uncomfortable and often adversarial experience of being sold. But as long as there's a gap between reality and fantasy, we can never grant our customer's wish for the perfect offer. After all, that unstated wish list will often include things like "at no cost," "taking no time," "requiring no effort," and "involving no risk"—things that no business can guarantee.

So what can we do about this inevitable gap between what they want and what we've got that forces them out of a posture of buying and us into a posture of selling? Fundamentally, there are two choices:

OPTION #1: GET BETTER AT SELLING

So what if people hate being sold? It still works, doesn't it? You can still close deals, make sales, and put food on the table for your kids. Besides, your prospects' desires aren't reasonable or fair anyway. Do they have any idea of the hurdles you've had to leap over to make your offer as good as it is today? Of course not, so they need guidance in the form of strong marketing and sales to help them realize that your offer really is the best thing for them. So you invest your time and resources in improving your ads, marketing copy, and conversion process.

OPTION #2: MAKE IT EASIER TO BUY

Instead of convincing people to go for something that isn't quite what they want, you focus on improving your offer, and making it ever closer to the ideal of what people are eager to buy. This takes a longer-term vision and a willingness to work harder today so that things can be easier tomorrow. This is the path of the Obvious Offer.

Now, obviously, this isn't really an either-or sort of decision; since no offer will ever be perfect and your prospects will never arrive with complete knowledge of the benefits you offer and the advantages you provide over the competition, there will always be an important role for both sales and marketing as part of the organization. And, particularly in the short term, it's a lot easier to sell better (which usually comes down to better words about your offer) than it is to improve what you're actually selling (which can involve substantial research and development investment).

Consider Amazon's recognition that customers will always want low prices, vast selection, and fast delivery. The company was committed to delivering on these dimensions from the very beginning—before they were actually all that good at it. I remember, for example, living in Israel in the late '90s and early 2000s. We would order books from Amazon and wait impatiently for the four to eight weeks that it took for the package to arrive. There was a long road to get from those shipping times to the two-hour delivery that you can now count on in some major cities. And with each incremental step on that road, Amazon's offer became a little bit more obvious.

In the same way, investing your resources in creating a more obvious offer will make it easier for you to sell and grow, and harder for your competitors to keep up. But before you can design a more obvious offer, you first need to get really clear on what your ideal customer actually wants—and figuring that out can be harder than you might expect!

Why You Can't Just Ask (Explicit vs. Implicit Desires)

For several years, I had a routine of waking up at the crack of dawn and walking to my neighborhood Starbucks. Every morning I would greet the barista behind the counter, and they would ask me what I wanted to drink. My answer: a tall Earl Grey tea, with coconut milk on the side—a drink that they dutifully and diligently prepared. It was a pleasant routine that eventually came to an end because of one simple fact: I was lying. The truth is that for the better part of two decades I've done my best to avoid caffeine, which Earl Grey tea contains in generous quantities. And I find that the flavor of coconut milk is too strong and distinctive for my taste. So why did I place the same order every morning for something that I didn't want? Simply because if I had asked for what I really wanted, I'd get a blank stare followed by those six words that nobody wants to hear: "I'm sorry, we can't do that."

You see, if I had my druthers, I'd be drinking an African rooibos red tea, which offers the rich flavor and consistency of black tea, but no caffeine. And my whitener of choice is macadamia milk, for reasons of flavor, texture, and health. Neither rooibos tea nor macadamia milk are on the menu at Starbucks, though, and I'm well-adjusted enough to know that when they ask what I want, what they really want to know is what I want *of the options that are available.*

This is why figuring out what your customers want isn't as simple as just asking them. Each of our wish lists has two columns on it: Column A is the stuff that we feel justified and reasonable in asking for, and column B is the stuff that we would never ask for out loud, and might not even consciously admit to ourselves. But even if we don't say it, and even if we don't realize it, it's still there—and to create a truly Obvious Offer, we must address both sides of that list. Consider the electric car company Tesla. Car buyers might ask in so many words for a car that is electric, has a long battery life, and handles well. Check, check, and check. But most wouldn't feel comfortable asking for a car that drives and parks itself, and will come to them when summoned. But Tesla understood that these features were on the list, and built them, even though it cost a fortune, and nobody would have even thought to ask for them.

EXPLICIT	IMPLICIT
Electric	Self-driving
Long battery life	Self-parking
Handles well	Comes when called

Or consider the wish list that makes up the feature set of Uber: "I want to press a button on my phone and instantly have a car appear. I want them to know that I like it quiet and air-conditioned, and for them to take the shortest route to get me to exactly where I need to go. And I don't want to pay much, or have to worry about the cost at all. Just charge my card, and I'll figure it out later." How much of that would you have felt comfortable asking of a taxi company before Uber?

So yes, by all means, start by asking your prospects what they want, and your customers what made them want to buy—that will help you populate the explicit list of things that they're looking for. That's where any marketing consultant worth their salt will tell you to start, and for good reason: It's where the low-hanging fruit of opportunity will be found. But while asking your customers can be a good start, it won't get you all the insight you need to design a truly Obvious Offer. For that, we need to loosen our mental constraints on what we imagine might be possible. To help you do that, I'll share three thought exercises: (1) Three Wishes for Your Ideal Customer, (2) The Perfect-World Guarantee, and (3) 10 Times More Obvious.

THREE WISHES FOR YOUR IDEAL CUSTOMER

My first exposure to Disney's classic movie *Aladdin* was when it came out in theaters in 1992. Since then I've watched the Robin Williams *tour de force* countless times, coming full circle to now watching it with my own children. That movie prompted millions of people to muse about what their wishes might be if they were to happen upon a magic lamp and genie of their own. You only get three, so you have to be strategic. Speaking for myself, I would say to the genie that "my first wish would be to always be in peak health, fitness, energy, and mental acuity"—which I rationalize is okay, because it's really providing details about a single wish rather than four separate ones!

It's a fun thought exercise to imagine the invocation of a supernatural genie relaxing the constraints on what might be possible. Your answer to the question of what you want in your new sedan will be very different if it is being asked by a genie as opposed to a car dealer! So let's invoke that thought exercise, and imagine what answers your prospects would give about the problem your offer is meant to solve or the delight that it is meant to create. Don't edit the list. Just make it as long and rich as you can. Don't worry about how impactful it would or wouldn't be yet, and don't worry about feasibility—in fact, the more outrageous the wishes, the better. You can brainstorm these ideas by answering questions like what...

...have your customers been asking for that you never thought you could deliver?

...do your customers love that you could double down on?

...are your competitors' practices that you could adopt?

...could you do to create more delight and better results?

...are the reasons you lose customers, and what could you do differently?

...are the annoyances that your customers experience that you could eliminate?

...would you do for your customers if time and money were no object?

The key to this exercise is to escape the constraints of "we can't do that," "that would never fly," and "that's not how it works"—there's a place for that sorting and analysis, but first we need to put on our "what-if hats" and engage in some blue-sky thinking. So block off some time, get your best people together, and have some fun brainstorming what your company would look like if you had a genie on your R & D team. And if inviting your hypothetical (or real) customer to wish for features and experiences doesn't bear fruit, there's another tack you might try: identifying your perfect-world guarantee.

THE PERFECT-WORLD GUARANTEE

There are only two reasons why anyone ever buys anything: They either want something that they don't have, or they have something that they don't want. Either way, it is only in rare cases that what we buy is actually the thing that we want; more often, we're buying whatever we perceive to be the means that will accomplish our ends—like Harvard Business School professor Theodore Levitt's famous line that "people don't want to buy a quarter-inch drill, they want to buy a quarter-inch hole!"

For entrepreneurs and marketers, however, it can be easy to lose sight of our customer's ultimate goal (the quarter-inch hole) and focus on the thing that is core to our expertise, and within our ability to provide (the quarter-inch drill). That's why it can be such a valuable exercise to remind ourselves of what the ultimate ends are that our customer wants to achieve. To borrow a phrase from Stanford University professor and *Tiny Habits* author BJ Fogg, "if you could wave a magic wand and make anything happen, what is the outcome that they ultimately want?" Then take the insight that comes from the answer to that question, and add another layer to it: Ask yourself, What would it take for you to actually guarantee that outcome?

If you'll allow me, let's digress for a moment about the value of a guarantee. I'm a big fan of powerful and creative guarantees of outcomes, but not for the reasons that most marketers think. Marketers tend to see guarantees as tools of "risk reversal" that take away the risk of spending time and money on something that doesn't work—and there is truth to that, particularly if you're looking to craft an Obvious Offer (a common question on a customer's wish list is, "Can you guarantee that it will work?"). But even more than that, I value guarantees as tools of organizational alignment;

they make it crystal clear to everyone on your team what you're on the hook to deliver.

Now, I'm not saying that you should or even could guarantee the ultimate results that your customers will experience, as there may be any number of things that are beyond your control to influence (How can I guarantee a quarter-inch hole without knowing what material you're trying to drill into?). But just as a thought exercise, ask yourself: If I were trying to guarantee the customer's ultimate outcome, what would I have to do in order to reliably make that happen? Whether you ultimately make that guarantee a part of your offer or not, this thought exercise is a good way of unearthing the wish list of things that could be evolved about your offer to make it more obvious.

11-STAR EXPERIENCES, 10X MORE OBVIOUS

If you've ever sat in a brainstorming session, you've probably experienced the phenomenon whereby the first idea might be interesting and against the grain, but then the next five suggestions are all variations on the same theme. This is because sometimes the hardest thing about innovation is getting past the frame of reference of what you've already built. Sometimes the easiest way to see your way to innovation is to pretend you're starting with a clean slate—instead of iterating on what you've already got, imagine that you're starting from scratch in approaching the problem.

Dan Sullivan, co-founder of Strategic Coach and author of books like *Who Not How*, explains this phenomenon under the headline that "10x is easier than 2x." In a nutshell, the idea is that our thinking will always struggle with the inertia of what we've already figured out, and default to variations on that theme. In response to the question of "How can I double (2x) my results?" we instinctively reach for incremental solutions: working harder, being more efficient, and getting more yield out of the approaches that we're already pursuing. But when asked to find ways to 10x our results, we sense that what we're doing probably won't produce such a disproportionate outcome, so we start with a mental blank slate, and explore how we might create a ten-times-better result.

Airbnb co-founder and CEO Brian Chesky uses a similar model to design viral products and experiences, called the "11-star experience." The idea is to think through what a five-star service would be like, and then extrapolate that out to eleven stars—not with the expectation that you could actually build whatever you imagine to be the ten- or eleven-star option, but to think and design to the extreme, and work backward to develop a delightful (read: obvious) experience. In the same vein, ask yourself what it would take to make your offer into an "11-star experience" that is 10x more obvious than it is today. Chasing down the trails of this thought exercise will help you arrive at interesting and novel ideas that might not otherwise come to mind.

Using this and the previous two exercises to create that wish list, you are now ready to take off the hat of creative visionary, and put on the hat of analyst and strategist who actually decides what to do first, second, and third as you evolve toward a more obvious offer.

Evolving Toward a More Obvious Offer

When we were expecting our second child, we realized that the not-quite-two-bedroom condo we were living in would be too small for our growing family, so we started house hunting. Eventually, we found a place that was within our budget in the neighborhood we liked that had the space we wanted, indoor garage parking (very important for Montreal winters!), a good-sized backyard, and central air. It checked all the boxes, so we bought it, but that doesn't mean it was perfect.

The layout was weird, the walls were covered in a gross-looking stucco, there was unattractive wall-to-wall carpeting, the upstairs bathroom was cramped and ugly, the backyard was a mess, and the whole place was way too dark. My wife and I made a list of all the renovations and improvements that we wanted to make, and quickly realized that the sum total of work we wanted done would have taken us well past my wife's delivery date, by which point we wanted to be comfortably settled into our new home, not to mention that the price tag attached to our total wish list was just a tiny bit outside of our budget. We asked questions like:

- Where would we get the best bang for our buck?
- What are the things that we couldn't live without?
- What are the things that would cost a lot more to do later vs. now?

We eventually settled on taking down some of the ground floor walls to create more space (great bang for buck), cleaning the stucco off the walls (couldn't live in a house that looked like it had worms crawling in the walls), and replacing the carpeting with hardwood floors (which would be hugely inconvenient to do later, since we'd have to move all our stuff out of the way). Everything else on our long wish list could wait until later.

You'll want to do the same sort of analysis with your Obvious Offer wish list. Fundamentally, what you're doing is weighing the cost and impact of each item on your list. If the list is short and the numbers are large, you can do this informally in your head, the way my wife and I did with the potential renovations to our new home. For a longer list, though, it helps to map them out on a cost vs. impact grid. You can go so far as to write the ideas out on Post-it notes, and put them up on a poster board to make a matrix, like this one:

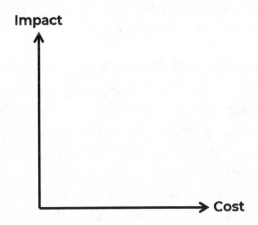

Seeing your ideas plotted on this grid, you can think differently about how, when, and whether to put them into action depending on the quadrant in which they're found:

HIGH IMPACT / LOW COST = LOW HANGING FRUIT. This is the territory of gold mines that you didn't realize were right under your nose: the opportunity to quickly and easily make your offer substantially more obvious to the customer. It's rare to have a lot of opportunities in this quadrant, but if the opportunities are there, you should move quickly to seize them—especially because if you don't, it's only a matter of time before your competitors will.

LOW IMPACT / LOW COST = INCREMENTAL IMPROVEMENT.
This is the stuff that's easy to do, but won't move the needle all that much. There are usually a lot of these ideas lying around, and it's easy for them to languish on the sidelines. You should dedicate a small amount of time and energy to making these changes on an ongoing basis, because the effects are cumulative—a compounding 1% improvement adds up over time, and not making these changes can add up to death by a thousand paper cuts.

HIGH IMPACT / HIGH COST = RESEARCH & DEVELOPMENT.
This quadrant is where most businesses drop the ball—the things that will take a lot of time and effort, but if you get them right it will be a big advantage in your favor. These aren't the opportunities to get you out of a jam (because they take too much time and money to act on), but they're the things that create sustained, long-term advantages for your business. You would be wise to allocate to the function of research and development as much time and energy as you can sustainably afford without a short-term return.

LOW IMPACT / HIGH COST = BAD IDEAS. This is the slush pile, the brain farts that emerge as by-products of otherwise fruitful brainstorming. Leave these ideas on your "not-to-do" list, but first examine the ideas closely to make sure you aren't conflating the flatout low impact of a bad idea with the short-term low impact of a potential R & D winner.

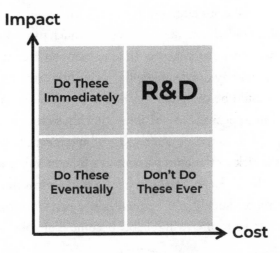

So there you have it: your prioritization plan for which opportunities to pursue first, second, and third in pursuit of a more obvious offer. But, as you can see, this isn't something that you do once, quickly, and mark as done. It's a process of continuous improvement that requires dedication and patience. The goal isn't to make your offer a million times better overnight, but rather to make it so that every week or month your offer gets just a little bit more obvious.

WILL IT REALLY BE BETTER?

No matter how much time and effort we put into planning and strategizing, we can never be 100% certain that those plans and strategies will yield the intended results. Sometimes the grandest gesture lands flat, the sincerely heartfelt gift isn't appreciated, and the *mot juste* just doesn't land. This is simply because we can only guess at what goes on inside the hearts and minds of others, including our ideal customers.

So as we make our efforts to plan, prioritize, and execute the enhancements intended to make our offer that much more obvious with every step, we must also take the time to test and measure whether our efforts are having the desired effect. Your first attempt at any improvement should be designed to validate your core assumptions as quickly and inexpensively as possible—quickly, so that you can pivot and iterate rapidly as the situation calls for, and inexpensively, so as to minimize the risk to the entrepreneur. It's Silicon Valley author and thinker Eric Ries's Lean Startup cycle of build, measure, learn, and repeat; the more quickly and frequently you can work through this cycle, the more your offer will reliably become more obvious.

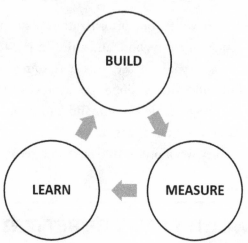

This sort of iteration usually happens in small bits and bites, following Jim Collins's dictum of firing bullets before cannonballs. Your offer probably won't become dramatically more obvious overnight, and that's fine. The goal is to make it just a bit more obvious each and every day. If you maintain a steady pace of improvement, you'll find that the improvements add up to a significant advantage.

JUST A LITTLE BIT MORE OBVIOUS

Jim and Bob are walking in the woods when they spot a brown bear. Jim puts down his pack and starts putting on his running shoes. Bob says to him, "Are you crazy? You can't outrun a brown bear!" Jim answers, "I don't have to outrun the bear; I just have to outrun you!" Now, Jim is clearly a terrible friend and human being, with the narcissistic self-explanatory urges of a Bond villain. But he has a point: you don't need to be the fastest creature in the forest; you just have to be fast enough to get ahead.

The same is true with Obvious Offers, which is important to keep in mind if you're staring down the disheartening barrel of a pages-long list of things to improve about your offer. While it's certainly a good ideal to aim for, your near-term goal isn't to create the most obvious offer that the world has ever seen. Rather, goal number one is to make your offer more obvious than the alternatives your prospects are weighing. Then, when you clear that hurdle, goal number two is to widen the gap, making your offer so much more of a no-brainer that it will be even harder for competitors to catch up with you. The further you widen that gap, the more obvious your offer will be, and the more effortless growing will become.

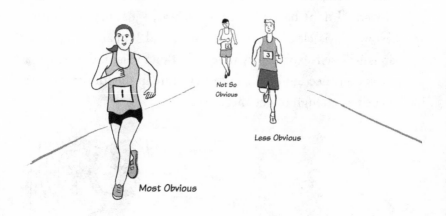

Not So
Obvious

Less Obvious

Most Obvious

Case Study: The Obvious Business Acceleration Program

I'll illustrate the ideas in this chapter with the process through which my Mirasee team and I created our flagship business coaching offer, called the ACES Business Acceleration Program. This program was designed from the ground up to be the Obvious Offer to our ideal customer, but you can apply the same thinking to reengineer an existing offer in your business in the same way.

Our ideal customer, remember, is a coach, consultant, speaker, author, or expert who is looking to grow their leverage, freedom, and impact through the vehicle of an online business. They typically find us while exploring the idea of creating an online course as a main driver of that business; the making and selling of online courses is the core expertise that I and my company are known for, so we're often found through books I've written on the subject like *Teach Your Gift*, and online training programs like our Course Business Masterclass (which are also designed to be Obvious Offers, but that would be a different case study!).

At each turn of our customer journey, there is a problem or need that people feel. We address that need, and that creates a new need for what comes next. People come to us asking whether an online course might be a good vehicle for them to grow their impact and income, and through our books and free training they find an answer. Assuming the answer is yes, they will often continue into one of our paid training programs, where they get the step-by-step instructions combined with coaching support that they need to build and launch their online course. We make it a priority to make sure they're profitable on the entire experience.

From there, they broaden their focus from just the online course to their entire expertise-driven business. That's the need that the ACES Business Acceleration Program is designed around. And as with all our offers, we start by asking ourselves what outcomes our customers would want guaranteed in a perfect world. In the case of ACES, their goal is very straightforward: they want to grow their business.

So we then asked ourselves what it would take for us to guarantee that every customer (who was a good fit to join the program) would succeed in growing their business. We made a long list of things that we would have to put on the table to be able to make that promise, and five absolute requirements emerged:

1. **EXPERTISE** – Access to top-tier strategists to create customized plans for business growth, and capitalization on the unique opportunities facing each of our client entrepreneurs.

2. **COACHING** – A team of highly skilled and trained business coaches, who work closely and individually with our client entrepreneurs to navigate obstacles and build forward momentum.

3. **ACCOUNTABILITY** – Systems and mechanisms to keep our client entrepreneurs' focus on the areas of greatest opportunity within their business, and flag our coaches when intervention is needed.

4. **COMMUNITY** – Since greatness is never achieved alone, the ACES program includes a robust community experience where entrepreneurs connect with, and are supported by, their peers.

5. **SERVICES** – High-skilled vendors in a variety of areas (from web design, to copywriting, to advertising, and everything in between) to implement key strategies for our clients.

The goal in designing all of this into the experience is to never have to say the words "I'm sorry, we can't do that." If I join the ACES program, will I get the strategic guidance that I need to grow my business? Yes. Will you coach me through challenges? Yes. Will you check in with me to keep me on task? Yes. Will you help me evaluate opportunities as they come up in my business? Yes. Will I be connected to other entrepreneurs like me? Yes. Will I have opportunities to network and learn? Yes. Can you do actual implementation work in my business, for the stuff that I don't have the expertise to do myself? Yes.

It wasn't easy, but knowing what needed to be included in the program for it to deliver on the results that our customers wanted (and that we do in fact guarantee), we set to work building all five of these components into the program (*ACES* is a clumsy acronym, with the *C* doing double duty for coaching and community). The effort was worthwhile; the program, which is only a few years old, currently supports over 150 client entrepreneurs, and membership increases with every cohort.

But that's not to say that we can rest on our laurels. The work is never done; we start a new cohort three times each year, and with each cohort we pilot-test new ways to improve the program and make it even easier and faster for our clients to get the results that they come to us for. In this way, the offer becomes more obvious with every cohort that we run, and we see this in the enrollment of the program. We often have a waiting list for people signed up to start close to half a year in advance.

Chapter Review

Wondering whether you caught every idea in this chapter? Or just looking to review? Here's a quick summary of the ideas that we covered here:

- Much of Amazon's success can be traced back to an obsessive focus on the things that will never change, and that people will always want: low prices, vast selection, and fast delivery. This is Amazon's formula for an Obvious Offer.

- Sales guru Jeffrey Gitomer is known for saying that people hate to be sold, but love to buy. The difference is that buying is claiming exactly what you want, whereas being sold to is being told that you can't have what you want, and should get something else instead.

- Having a perfectly Obvious Offer means never having to say "I'm sorry, we can't do that." This reduces the need to get better at selling by making it easier for people to buy.

- It takes time to create an Obvious Offer, because the first few attempts to move in that direction won't be all that impressive. For example, Amazon's commitment to fast delivery in the early days still took a pretty long time.

- Every customer has two columns on their wish list: column A is the stuff that we feel justified and reasonable in asking for, and column B is the stuff that we would never ask for out loud, and might not even consciously admit to ourselves that we want.

- A fun thought exercise to get to the deep desires on your customer's wish list is to ask them, in the context of the problem you solve, what wishes they would ask a magical genie to grant.

- Another exercise is to explore what outcomes your customer would want guaranteed if you could wave a magic wand and make anything happen.

- Once you have your list, you must prioritize which improvements to make first, second, and third. You can do this by plotting all the options on a matrix of cost vs. impact. Start with the low-hanging fruit (high impact / low cost), spend some time regularly working on incremental improvements (low impact / low cost), and put long-term resources into research and development (high impact / high cost).

- Remember that everything you build will be based on an assumption that people will like it, but the assumption won't always be true. So run small tests to make sure you're right, using the Lean Startup methodology of build, measure, learn, and repeat.

- Your short-term goal doesn't need to be creating the most obvious offer that the world has ever seen; it's enough to be just a bit more obvious than your competition, and then slowly improve from there.

CHAPTER 3
Cultivate Your
Resonant Identity

*"We all prefer to do business with people
that we know, like, and trust."*

—BOB BURG

MERCEDES OR BMW? Walmart or Target? Grey Goose or Belvedere? McDonald's or Burger King? Harvard or Yale? Every day, we're faced with countless decisions like these, choosing between two (or more) companies that do pretty much exactly the same thing, in the same way, for the same price.

Consider the Four Seasons and Ritz-Carlton hotel chains. Both are premium, luxury brands that promise best-in-class service and accommodations at a hefty price tag. Both have even had books published about their founding and ethos. If you've never stayed at either, they're pretty much completely interchangeable. But if you've had some experience with either or both brands, you probably have a clear preference for one or the other.

Your preference can't be reduced to a pros-and-cons list, and you may not even be able to articulate your rationale for caring one way or the other. But you do care, on an instinctive and gut level—one choice just "feels right." That feeling comes down to a lot of things that have the rare distinction in the marketing world of literally going without saying.

What Goes Without Saying

If you ever find yourself next to a charismatic Asian gentleman on a business class flight out of Toronto, ask him what he does for a living. If he smiles and says that his job is to "seek and destroy margin-sucking maggots," you're sitting next to Ken Wong, the Canadian Marketing Hall of Legends inductee and Distinguished Professor of Marketing at Queen's University's Smith School of Business. I had the privilege of sitting in Wong's class over a decade ago, where he leveraged his speaking and showmanship skills to drive home the finer points of marketing and branding.

At one memorable point, he held up a nondescript piece of plastic and asked us what we could tell him about it. The object was small and the lecture hall was large, so most of us couldn't even see what it was, let alone tell him something meaningful about it. He put the object away behind the lectern, and added, "What if I told you that it was made by Fisher-Price?" Our hands shot in the air, eager to volunteer insights about the object we couldn't even see. If it was made by Fisher-Price, then we all knew two things about it: first, that it was a toy designed for small children, and second, that it was safe. Sight unseen, we all knew that it would be free of small parts, lead paint, or anything else that we wouldn't want a toddler getting their hands (or mouth) on.

Brands are a mental shortcut that we use when we don't have the time, inclination, or expertise to look under the proverbial hood.

A strong brand can inform us about who a company services, what their product is likely to do, and even how much we should pay for it, as explained by this excerpt from the article "Better Branding: The Gift that Keeps on Giving!" by branding expert Re Perez:

> To demonstrate the power of brands which shape expectations, Tim Calkin, Associate Professor at the Kellogg School of Management, conducted a simple study with MBA students. He first asked the students what they would expect to pay for a pair of good quality 18 Karat gold earrings with 3 Karat diamonds. He asked a second group of students how much they would pay for the same earrings? Only this time he added the words "from Tiffany." He asked the third group the same question, but this time changed "from Tiffany" to "Wal-Mart."
>
> The results were striking. The average price for the unbranded earrings was $550, with Tiffany's branding the average price increased to $873, a jump of 60%. With Wal-Mart the price expectation fell to just $81, a decline of 85% from the unbranded earrings and a decline of 91% from the Tiffany branded earrings.

TIFFANY & CO.   Walmart

$550 $873 $81

To understand the lesson of these results, we must remember that the subjects of the study were not jewelers examining the actual earrings, but rather MBA students who had to make a judgment based on a brief description. Offhand, most people don't know what a pair of earrings' weight in gold is worth, or what 3-karat diamonds cost—or even whether the answer to that question would be a price or a range of possible prices! But we do have enough exposure to the world to have a sense of what jewelry usually costs, that things at Tiffany cost more, and that Walmart's catalog is designed around their promise of everyday low prices. And even if the MBA students do know what a pair of good-quality 18-karat gold earrings with 3-karat diamonds should cost, the brand might cause them to question what they think they know. High-quality gold earrings aren't the sort of thing that you'd find at Walmart, so maybe there are different kinds of gold and diamonds? Or maybe they forgot the part of the description that said "good quality" and assumed that at Walmart it must be gold-plated or something? Whatever information was explicitly given, the brand conveyed a lot more information that never had to be said—for better, and sometimes for worse.

If it comes in a distinctive Tiffany Blue Box, you can count on it being prestigious and expensive. If Walmart sells it, it won't cost all that much. If it's made by Apple, you can count on sleek design and impeccable attention to detail. If they graduated from Harvard, you know that they're either rich or ultra-remarkable. And if it comes in a brown paper bag sporting McDonald's golden arches, you know it isn't good for you. These are things that we all "know," even if we don't have any specific information to support it. (How can a salad be bad for you? No idea, but if it's from McDonald's, I'm pretty sure it is!)

There are many things that strangers must come to know, understand, and believe before they will be ready to become customers—specific things about the features and benefits of your offer, and its suitability for them and their needs. Conveying these things is done as part of laying out your Intuitive Path, which we'll explore in the next chapter. The truth is, though, that a lot of buying decisions come down to the customer's gut feeling that you're "their kind of company." When that gut feeling exists, it is your true ace in the hole, earning you the benefit of the doubt in the face of uncertainty, and galvanizing your customers as evangelists and defenders. To understand it, we'll explore the traits that make deeply charismatic leaders so compelling. But first, a quick aside.

RESONANT IDENTITIES AND PERSONALITY BRANDS

As we dive into the traits of Resonant Identities, many of the traits and examples we'll explore will seem to apply particularly well to personality brands. This is because human beings are wired to connect with other human beings, and that's the reason why it is simply easier to cultivate a Resonant Identity for a personality brand. That doesn't mean it can't be done for other brands, and many brands do have clear and specific Resonant Identities. That said, as I write this book I am guided by two principles:

1. **RELEVANCE TO MY READERS,** most of whom are coaches, consultants, speakers, authors, and experts. In other words, personality brands.

2. **SIMPLICITY AND CLARITY,** and it is a lot simpler and clearer to understand these ideas when talking about the character and traits of specific people, which again means personality brands.

So does the content of this chapter apply to businesses that aren't centered around a personality? Yes, absolutely. Are there good examples of Resonant Identities that are companies rather than people? Yes, there are many (Harley Davidson, Dollar Shave Club, Poo~Pourri, etc.), though to be fair, there's usually some component of a celebrity leader personality associated with the brand (Apple and Steve Jobs, Tesla and Elon Musk, Starbucks and Howard Schultz, Patagonia and Yvon Chouinard, Whole Foods Market and John Mackey, SPANX and Sara Blakely, etc.).

But while all that is true, much of the chapter will center on personality brands, as those examples will be both the clearest and the most relevant to the majority of my readers. Now that you have read this little disclaimer, let's turn our attention back to the traits found in all deeply charismatic leaders.

What Makes a Hero?
(Ingredients of Charismatic Leadership)

Superman isn't the popular hero in the 21st century that he was in the 20th. You might be tempted to attribute the character's decline to the rise of Iron Man and the Marvel Cinematic Universe (MCU)—after all, the franchise accounted for over two thirds (and $30 billion) of the fifty top-grossing superhero movies of the last couple of decades. But the decline of

Superman extends further. Even comparing heroes from the same (currently second-tier) marquee DC Comics, movies featuring the Last Son of Krypton did worse at the box office than Wonder Woman movies (a newcomer to the silver screen) and grossed less than half of what Batman movies did. The conclusion is clear: Superman is on the outs.

But despite all that, he remains the quintessential superhero. A Google image search for "superhero" shows as much: While the results include modern favorites like Iron Man, Captain America, and the like, over half of the top images either show Superman, or are Superman-esque (generic superhero in a blue suit and red cape, or ripping open a shirt to reveal a superhero suit underneath). Why then, regardless of what movies we might be especially excited to see, does Superman remain the embodiment of what a superhero is? Our resonance with Superman's identity is the product of two factors:

1. **RELATABILITY.** Despite the fact that Superman is literally from another world, there is much of him in the experience of most people, and particularly the sort of person who has historically gravitated to superhero comics. Superman's alter ego Clark Kent is mild-mannered, nerdy, and nondescript—as invisible as many comic book fans often feel. Despite being the most powerful man in the world, the woman he loves doesn't even know who he is.

Relatability is what makes us feel connected to a person, character, or brand ("you're just like me"), but alone it doesn't make for a Resonant Identity. For that, we need another ingredient...

2. **ASPIRATION.** Superman is in many ways "just like us," but of course he is also "faster than a speeding bullet, more

powerful than a locomotive, and can leap tall buildings in a single bound." He is also good and wise; while the rest of us may occasionally succumb to temptation and veer from the straight and narrow, he never wavers. As much as we can relate to the person that Superman is, he also embodies the traits that we aspire to possess.

There's a dynamic tension between relatability and aspiration in that drifting too far toward one will compromise the other; if you're too much like me then there's not much left to aspire to, and if you're too aspirational of an example there won't be enough for me to relate to. Right in the middle is the beautiful equilibrium of "you're just like me AND you're who I want to be when I grow up"—and therein lies a truly Resonant Identity.

That balance of relatability and aspiration is the key to the loyal audiences amassed by every charismatic leader and brand, such as business thinkers (Tim Ferriss, Scott Galloway), musicians (Lady Gaga, Bono), political leaders (John McCain, Alexandria Ocasio-Cortez), and media personalities (Oprah Winfrey, Jay Leno).

	RELATABILITY ("you're just like me")	**ASPIRATION** ("you're who I want to be when I grow up")
TIM FERRISS	We both care about business, productivity, and living our best lives.	He pushes himself to the limit in pursuit of excellence.
SCOTT GALLOWAY	We're both smart, funny, and have strong opinions.	He is insightful and unafraid to call it like he sees it.
LADY GAGA	We both feel vulnerable about who we are.	She is talented, successful, and brave.
BONO	We both care about the environment and social causes.	He is talented and super successful.
JOHN MCCAIN	We both care about honor and decency.	He is a war hero and leader.
ALEXANDRIA OCASIO-CORTEZ	We're both inner-city tough and care about people like us.	She is sharp, poised, and fearless.
OPRAH WINFREY	We're both vulnerable, kind, and authentic.	She is brilliant, successful, and stands up for what she believes in.
JAY LENO	We're both decent, down-to-earth, and dyslexic.	He is funny and successful.

No identity is resonant for everyone, but for the right people, Resonant Identities strike the perfect balance of relatability and aspiration. As another example, and at the risk of stirring the political pot, consider Presidents Barack Obama and Donald Trump. Each president's core constituencies clearly found him to be deeply resonant—to each of those groups, their president embodies the perfect balance of "you're just like me, and you're who I want to be when I grow up."

Marketing and business growth become so much more effortless when your audience is presold on the idea that you're "their kind of person," which is a function of these two ingredients (relatability and aspiration). So now let's explore what it takes to create that Resonant Identity for your business.

RELATABILITY ("YOU'RE JUST LIKE ME")

Before you can point the way to a better future (which on some level is the promise of any product or service), your customers need to feel that you understand them. And that understanding comes from the things that you share with them, that most people don't, what my friend and networking expert Jayson Gaignard likes to call "uncommon commonalities." These are the things that you and your target customer have in common, but don't share with the rest of the world—and that's what makes them special. These commonalities can be about your values, interests, challenges, or quirks:

CORE VALUES. One of the most important points of connection between a person and a brand are the values that they both share. What do they believe in and care about that you do as well? What are the tenets of behavior that you would never waver from, no matter what? I'm not talking about the posters of platitudes hanging on many office walls, but rather a set of values that are carefully defined, meaningfully understood, and always top of mind for every person in your organization. Identifying and living those values for your organization is beyond the scope of this book (and if you want to learn more about how to do it, a great resource is Patrick Lencioni's book *The Advantage*), but if you have them, they're a great point of meaningful connection with your customers.

INTERESTS AND PASSIONS. No matter how passionate you are about your work, there's more to you than what you do for a living. The same is true for your customers, and in those other dimensions of your identity and theirs may be an opportunity to find common ground. Maybe you're both passionate about exercise, or art, or sustainable living. Maybe you're both parents of high school–aged children. Maybe you share a fascination with travel. There's a reason why it's an old trope that when a salesperson walks into an office they look at the photos on the desk for an anchor of commonality: "Is that your son? My son is about the same age as yours, so we have that in common!"

STRUGGLES AND CHALLENGES. Not all commonalities are pleasant, and often the ones we wish we didn't share are the most resonant. Consider former Vice President Joe Biden, who, as I write this, is the Democratic candidate for president (and by the time you're reading this will have either won or lost the election); he lost his wife and young daughter in a car crash in 1972, and lost one of his sons to brain cancer in 2015. This experience of loss is an important part of the identity that makes him resonant to many who have lost loved ones, particularly in a time when hundreds of thousands of Americans have been lost to the COVID-19 pandemic. If there is a struggle or challenge that you and your ideal customer both have experience with, it can be a powerful point of connection. Just be careful not to undermine the aspirational part of the Resonant Identity; for example, if you're a business expert, then it's okay to share business setbacks, as long as they happened in the past!

QUIRKS AND IDIOSYNCRASIES. Consider this a catchall bucket for anything that you share with your ideal customer that hasn't already been covered. Maybe you're an introvert, or a fan of a particular sport or team, or spent time in the military—anything that you and your ideal customer have in common with each other (but not with most other people) is a potential point of connection.

Your time and energy would be well spent making a list of the core values, interests and passions, struggles and challenges, and quirks and idiosyncrasies that you and your ideal customers share. They are all potential points of connection, and key ingredients to establishing that quality of relatability that is an important part of your Resonant Identity.

ASPIRATION
("YOU'RE WHO I WANT TO BE WHEN I GROW UP")

Relatability is important, but it isn't enough. If all you've got is relatability, then you'd make a great friend, but not necessarily a great leader. The second piece of the Resonant Identity equation is aspiration: In addition to being like them, you also represent something that they aspire to, and want to eventually become. Usually tying into the transformation promised by your Obvious Offer, these points of aspiration can be along the lines of what you have created (outcomes and experience), what you can do (competencies and capabilities), or the way you behave in the world (core values):

OUTCOMES AND EXPERIENCE (WHAT YOU HAVE CREATED). As we explored in the previous chapter, nobody buys anything unless there's something that they want but don't have, or something that they have but don't want. In other words, they aspire to an "after picture" that is different from the way things look for them right now. If you can credibly offer that "after picture," then you should have many examples to showcase of what that picture looks like—maybe your own life and story, and hopefully the case studies of your clients. So paint and showcase that extended picture for your ideal customers; in what ways do you and your past clients have the outcomes and experiences that your prospects aspire to?

COMPETENCIES AND CAPABILITIES (WHAT YOU CAN DO). Whereas some transformations come strictly in the "done for you" variety, in many cases the way we'll get the outcomes that we want is by gaining the ability to do it ourselves. You and your brand should be the archetype of capability that your customers are looking to acquire for themselves ("when we're done, you'll be able to do this as well as I can"). So what are the skills and abilities that you have and can showcase that are aspirational to your ideal customers?

CORE VALUES (HOW YOU BEHAVE). We circle back to core values, because they are both core to who we are and what we resonate with, and they continue to be aspirational. Unlike Superman, we all falter from time to time, and look to examples of how we will show up in the world when we are better, stronger, and wiser. Even after his death, Senator John McCain is still appreciated and respected by many for the way in which he defended his opponent, Barack Obama, from racist attacks. That level of honor and integrity is rarely seen in modern politics, and (for the right person) is an aspirational value.

You've already made a list of the points of relatability on which you can connect with your ideal customer. Now create a second list that includes the outcomes that you've created, the things you can do, and the ways in which you behave that are aspirational to your ideal customers. These two lists are the ingredients of your Resonant Identity.

$$\begin{array}{r} POINTS\ OF\ RELATABILITY \\ +\quad POINTS\ OF\ ASPIRATION \\ \hline RESONANT\ IDENTITY \end{array}$$

But of course, if you want your ideal customers to resonate with your identity, the lists can't just sit in a drawer! Your Resonant Identity must permeate every aspect of your communication so that whatever part of what you do people are exposed to, they come away with that clear sense that you're "their kind of person."

Resonance and Authenticity

My organization follows a somewhat unusual process for hiring. It starts out conventionally enough, with a "help wanted" notice circulated on job boards, through our networks, and to our community. That job ad will point to an application form that asks a few screening questions about the candidate's expertise for the role, followed by a short technical exercise. If the candidate's application passes muster, they're invited to complete a second-round application, answering questions about how they would handle semi-hypothetical scenarios that they might face in the role. Interesting second-round applications are invited to do an exercise simulating the actual work that they would do on the job. Strong exercises lead to a battery of assessments, and the candidate provides three references who can vouch for their character and work ethic. Only if the entire package looks good will they be invited to an interview, and at no point will they be asked to provide a resume.

This unorthodox and rigorous process sits in sharp contrast with the way hiring works in many organizations, and the way I did it when I started my first business decades ago. Back then, the "help wanted" notice would invite people to submit a resume, which I would then discuss when them in an interview. Relevant and interesting work experience plus cogent answers to interview questions would lead to a job offer. This version seems straightforward and time-tested... so why change things? Because of the mountains of research that show it simply doesn't work; the data is clear that how well hiring managers expect a candidate to perform has no correlation whatsoever with how good of a job they actually do once hired. If you think about it, it isn't surprising. A hundred thousand years of human history, plus millions of years of primate evolution, have exquisitely equipped us to do many things, but quickly sizing up someone's work ethic and skill at insurance adjusting isn't one of them!

On the other hand, we have great skill for quickly assessing whether a stranger is someone with whom we'd enjoy socializing, and who can be trusted: in other words, whether they're "our kind of person." And what are we looking for? You guessed it: the two traits of relatability ("you're just like me") and aspiration ("you're who I want to be when I grow up"). This instinctive barometer of resonance is both a blessing and a curse to marketers and entrepreneurs, because it means that your ideal customers will be exquisitely attuned to indications of resonance, as well as indications that there's a gap between what you believe and what you say.

The upshot here is that these two traits aren't things that you can fake, which is why a Resonant Identity can be cultivated, but not crafted. The points of relatability and points of aspiration have to be true to who you really are and what you really care about—if they're simply affectations, I guarantee that not only will this not work for you, but also that it will backfire. So dig for the things that are true about yourself, and make sure you are living your values; only then will you be ready for them to permeate the image that you project and the way in which you communicate with the world.

THE COURAGE TO LET YOUR FREAK FLAG FLY

Clearly identifying the points of authentic relatability and aspiration that make up your Resonant Identity is only half the battle. The rest comes in actually communicating those things to your ideal customer. The good news is that, as we explored earlier, people are exquisitely attuned to pick up on clues that you're "their kind of person," or that you aren't. So start intentionally laying out those clues, through your voice (how you talk), message (what you say), and actions (what you do):

VOICE (HOW YOU TALK). Do you sound like a vanilla corporate entity, or like a real person? If it's the latter, then your voice by definition will have distinctive qualities—such as the cadence and pitch of your speech (think Barack Obama's slow rhythm and long pauses), your use or avoidance of profanity (for example, Gary Vaynerchuk or Mark Manson), words that connote special meaning when you say them (like Lady Gaga referring to her fans as "Little Monsters"), and even the mood and tone in which you speak (everything that comes out of Southwest Airlines sounds like it is said with a smile). These are all clues that people will latch onto as they look for resonance.

MESSAGE (WHAT YOU SAY). The positions that you take, the considerations to which you give weight, and the stories that you tell all speak volumes about who you are and what you care about. Most businesses have stories, anecdotes, and ways of being that they instinctively know will land well with their ideal customers. Those are often the things that they are reluctant to share, out of fear that people who aren't their ideal customer might hear because they won't like it in the same way. Consider how politicians sound different when speaking to their base vs. to the mainstream media, but the difference is that you don't need to win a popular vote; you just need to win the hearts and minds of your ideal customers.

ACTIONS (WHAT YOU DO). It's true that in many cases, actions speak louder than words. Even more important than what you say is what you actually do: what policies you enact, stands you take, causes you support, and limbs you choose to go out on. Putting your time, energy, and money where your mouth is makes an enormous difference in a world in which talk has become very cheap, and lip service to the cause of the day is part of the boilerplate of many marketers. Actions matter, and must be chosen with care and intentionality, to reflect the values that you truly hold dear.

Consider these three categories of voice, message, and actions for any brand whose identity is deeply resonant for their audience, and you'll find one thing in common: courage. They all know that letting their freak flag fly won't necessarily be well received by everyone that they meet, and that resonating with their ideal customer means *not* resonating with others. Resonant Identities are usually polarizing; for any truly Resonant Identity, in addition to their loyal audience there is probably also a large contingent of people who *don't* like them. That's par for the course, and something you have to be willing to accept as you pursue this path—not actively offending people (although some might go that far), but definitely being okay with some people not jiving with you and your message. The choice to cultivate a Resonant Identity is the decision that a strong and deep connection with the right people is better than a tepid comfort with everybody.

Case Study: Why You Might Find Resonance with... Me

"It seemed like a good idea at the time." That's what I'm thinking right now that it's time to write this chapter's case study illustrating the principles of a Resonant Identity with myself. This is very uncomfortable, not only because of the inherent challenge of turning the microscope around on yourself, but also because the mild-mannered Canadian in me much prefers to be the teacher sitting beside you and pointing to ideas rather than the showman with a spotlight on himself. But, in the interest of continuing our case study to help you understand the ideas of this book, I'll take a deep breath, grit my teeth, and proceed.

We must start with our ideal customer, because there is no such thing as an objectively resonant identity, just one that is resonant to the particular people you look to serve. For me and my business, if you recall, those people are coaches, consultants, speakers, authors, and experts. She is likely a well-educated woman in her mid-fifties who leans spiritual and liberal. So in what ways does she find me relatable, and what have I done that is aspirational to her?

It starts with the way that I talk and think, which you've seen over the past few chapters. Something about my style is interesting, engaging, and resonant for you—otherwise you probably wouldn't still be reading! You like the mix of big-picture ideas with well-laid-out strategy, illustrated with anecdotes and examples ranging from Renaissance art to TV sitcoms. And you appreciate that I'm not a fan of bombastic promises that "you too can be a bazillionaire if you just master my system." My customers appreciate that I put my kids first, share stories about them, and rarely work past 4 p.m., which is when they get out from day care and kindergarten. They appreciate that I enjoy popular science books, am deeply interested in education reform, and disproportionately like writing with a really good pen. They relate to the fact that I'm not an uber-charismatic, larger-than-life Tony Robbins-esque dynamo. I'm just a deeply motivated, slightly smart, and slightly awkward introvert who believes in the work that I do and the people that I get to serve.

And yet, despite being a guy that they can relate to and see themselves in, there are also some things about me that are aspirational, at least in the context of online course and business building, the area in which they look to me for guidance. Without bragging, the simple fact is that our online courses boast industry-leading completion and success rates. We've generated tens of millions of dollars selling online courses and coaching, and trained thousands of people to grow their online businesses in the same way.

These points of relatability and aspiration come across in the voice and language that I use, and are articulated in the stories that I share. They are codified and represented in the content that we publish, the ways that we work, and the experiences that we create.

Now, to be clear, my identity isn't resonant with everyone, but it is resonant to the people who are our kind of people, and that's the whole point. For example, consider the unorthodox hiring process that I described earlier in this chapter. The people who are a good fit for our culture and organization tend to like it; they report finding it interesting and even refreshing. They appreciate the challenge, respect that we're looking for a genuine best fit, and like that they learn something about themselves through the exercises and assessments. But not everyone feels that way; occasionally, we get comments like this one, left on a hiring application by a not-so-good-fit candidate the same day that I write these words:

> *Too much effort for a possible zero return. You pay, I work. No other terms are acceptable. This is demeaning. Go find a monkey to do your work. Top quality people are hired on the spot by CEOs. You obviously are not looking for a top-quality person.*

Clearly, I'm not his "kind of person," and he isn't mine. That's fine, and kind of the point—you'll never please everybody, but you should aim to amplify the parts of yourself that will be resonant with the right people, and push the others away.

Chapter Review

Wondering whether you caught every idea in this chapter? Or just looking to review? Here's a quick summary of the ideas that we covered here:

- Every day we decide between seemingly identical companies, and our choice often comes down to a simple gut feeling that one or the other option just "feels right." That feeling comes down to brand: the things that we "know" without them having to be said.

- There are two ingredients that make up a Resonant Identity: relatability ("you're just like me") and aspiration ("you're who I want to be when I grow up").

- All charismatic leaders and brands successfully walk the tightrope held in balance by these two traits of relatability and aspiration.

- Relatability is about the things that you share with your ideal customer, but not with most of the rest of the world. These uncommon commonalities can be about your values, interests, challenges, or quirks.

- Aspiration is about the things that your ideal customer wants to achieve that you already have, in terms of outcomes and experience (what you have created), competencies and capabilities (what you can do), and core values (how you behave).

- A Resonant Identity can't be faked; it has to be authentically real; otherwise, people will quickly see through the charade.

- The points of relatability and aspiration that make up your Resonant Identity can be communicated through voice (how you talk), message (what you say), and actions (what you do).

- Remember that Resonant Identities are usually polarizing; in addition to their loyal audience, there is probably also a large contingent of people who *don't* like them.

CHAPTER 4
Lay Out Your Intuitive Path

"Leadership is the art of getting someone else to do something
you want done because he wants to do it."

—DWIGHT EISENHOWER

I'VE ALWAYS ENJOYED WALKING, and Montreal is
a pedestrian-friendly city with great public transportation, so I was
able to get by for most of my life without a car. But in my early thirties, with a baby on the way, it was time for a change. My wife and I
bought our first car: a pre-owned and refurbished Mercedes B200.
The process for finding and making that purchase was... less than
smooth. First we had to narrow down from the broader universe of
cars to what would fit in our budget and match our style. We browsed
websites, looked at pictures, and read reviews. Once we settled on the
make and model that seemed right, we searched for a vendor and
found a couple. Since my wife and I aren't car people, we decided
to play it safe and buy a refurbished vehicle from the Mercedes-
Benz dealer. So we made an appointment, showed up, and took a
test drive. Then the negotiations began. Oh, the negotiations—they

were everything you'd imagine from every stereotype about the used car buying process. First "make me an offer," then "let me talk to my manager," and then after we had agreed on a price and signed the initial paperwork, the string of upsells. It was not a fun experience, nor one I'd care to repeat.

Our second car, six years later, was the blue Tesla model 3, which we still drive today, and the buying experience couldn't have been more different. We knew we wanted electric, and Tesla was more or less the only serious game in town, so we browsed over to Tesla.com. We reserved an appointment to do a test drive, showed up, enjoyed the ride, and thanked them for their time. Later that week, from the comfort of our living room couch, we opened the website again and began the purchase process. We selected the features that we wanted, all clearly marked with the associated costs. If a feature raised the price more than we wanted, we could navigate back and experiment with different configurations. When we were done, we put in a credit card for the deposit, and the order was complete. All that was left was to show up at the dealership a few weeks later to pick up the car—no muss, no fuss.

Compare these two buying experiences: one tortuous, and one smooth. Both were ultimately successful (I bought both cars!), but how much more motivated did I need to be to get through the two processes, how easily could I have abandoned one versus the other, and how likely am I to be a repeat buyer for the two brands? The answers to these questions are driven by the degree to which each business has (or hasn't) laid out an Intuitive Path for me to follow from idea to sale.

The Path from Stranger to Sale

If you've designed an Obvious Offer and cultivated a Resonant Identity, both of which are in alignment with your ideal customer, then you can trust that people want to buy what you're selling, and you're the person that they want to buy it from. That said, before getting to a place where they're ready to invest a substantial amount of time, money, and energy in anything, there are things that your future customer needs to know, understand, and believe: about the broader opportunity in which you operate, about themselves, and of course about you and your offer.

ABOUT THE OPPORTUNITY. Before anything else, people need to believe that the problem they're looking to solve is actually solvable. This may seem obvious, but unless people are actively looking for a solution, it can't be taken as given. We sometimes have persistent problems that have dropped from the top of our priorities (a problem has been downgraded from acute to chronic). In that scenario, some part of us has given up on the idea of the problem actually being solvable, and we've externalized responsibility as to why that is the case; relationships don't work because of the people around us, we can't get on top of our finances because the system is rigged against us, and we're stuck with our weight because of our genes—in all cases, we find a rationalization for why it's not our fault and there's nothing we can do about it. That being the case, before your future customer can even entertain the idea of buying a solution to their problem, they need to be open to the possibility of the problem being solvable. This takes a shift in worldview, and it is the first thing that you as entrepreneur need to impart.

ABOUT THEMSELVES. Disbelief comes in waves. The first is about the problem: "No, it can't be solved; this is just how it is." Once you dispel that, there's a new defense to overcome: "Okay, yes, I see how this can work for some people (out there, in the world)... but that doesn't mean it will work for me. Because I'm different. I'm special." This is where you need to show that not only is the problem solvable for people in general, but also specifically for people just like the ideal customer you're trying to attract: someone in their situation, with their same circumstances, challenges, and peculiarities. It's only after you show them definitively that a solution is eminently available to people just like them that they are ready to learn about you and your offer.

ABOUT YOU AND YOUR OFFER. Once your prospect is ready to learn about the specific thing that you're offering, there's a lot that they want to know: What does it include? How does it work? How long does it last? What outcomes will it produce? What does it cost? What results do you guarantee? These are just a few of the many, many questions that they'll ask. But behind all these questions, there are three broad categories of things that they really need to understand: relevancy ("why this?"), credibility ("why you?"), and urgency ("why now?"):

- RELEVANCY, I.E. "WHY THIS?" – How does your offer address the opportunity that they face and the need that they experience? Why is it the best option for getting what they want? Much of this ties back to your Obvious Offer, and needs to be communicated to the ideal prospect before they can become your ideal customer.

- CREDIBILITY, I.E. "WHY YOU?" – What makes you the most trustworthy vendor to buy from? What about your credentials, case studies, and guarantee structures will make them feel most comfortable? This is the Resonant Identity – why will they want to learn from you? It's not enough for you to have the answer; they need to know it too.

- URGENCY, I.E. "WHY NOW?" – Why do they need to do this now, rather than at some point in the future? What is the reason for acting now, today, before other priorities obscure their view? Along with the rest of the obviousness of your offer and the resonance of your identity, you also need to communicate why now is the time to act.

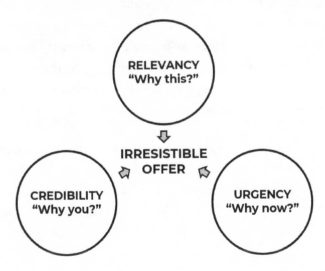

All of these things must be communicated to your ideal prospect before they will be ready to become your ideal customer. The process of imparting that knowledge, instilling that understanding, and conveying those beliefs is the path that strangers must follow to become customers. Your choice is whether that path will be tortuous and fraught (like my pre-owned Mercedes buying experience), or smooth and intuitive (like with Tesla). The latter is accomplished by aligning your business with your prospective customer's expectations and intuitions about what next step they should take at any given point, like...

> ...the next thing they want to read or hear or see from you...
> ...the next step you want them to take on a journey...
> ...the next thing you want them to invest in (whether it's their first investment with you, or the next one in a long and escalating series)...

...the more the next step you want them to take aligns with what feels logical and right and intuitive to them, the smoother that path will be. In this chapter we'll break down exactly how to create that smooth and logical flow of experience to create a Demand Narrative, which is the story that helps your customer connect the dots between their needs and your offer.

Important Note: The following sections summarize key ideas that usually take hours to explain and illustrate. If you would like more details on the mechanics of laying out your Intuitive Path, you are invited to attend a free Effortless Business Growth companion online workshop. Reserve your spot at our next workshop at Effortless.Rocks/workshop.

YOUR MARKETING *MISE-EN-PLACE*

When my son turned four, we went to the LEGO Store to choose his present. After a few minutes of wandering around the brightly colored displays and models, he made his decision: the BOOST Creative Toolbox, which is basically a kit to build your own LEGO robot, that you then connect via app to a tablet, and program with instructions. I told him that he would probably need help building it (the box indicated it was for ages seven through twelve, but I don't take those recommendations too seriously), and he suggested that we could build it together. That sold me, so we brought it home and opened the box to build it as a family. And, to be perfectly honest, I was a little apprehensive about the project; 847 pieces add up to a lot of opportunities for something to get lost and for someone to get frustrated.

But LEGO did a great job with the packaging. Those 847 pieces were grouped into over a dozen small, individually labeled bags, so that you didn't have to find and sort all those pieces to get started. They were presorted, so we could dive straight into the fun.

I can only surmise that the LEGO design team found inspiration here from the world of professional chefs; whereas amateurs in the kitchen will find and slice up ingredients as they're called for in the recipe (leading to delays, and some things being overcooked), professionals know to start with a *mise-en-place*. Literally translated from French as "putting in place" or "everything in its place", the *mise-en-place* is the collection of small bowls and containers filled with pre-chopped vegetables, pre-grated cheese, and other prepared ingredients. Professional chefs have a *mise-en-place* ready before they ever begin to cook so that they can focus their energies on the combinations of those ingredients and the timing of the steps of preparation that unlock the most interesting flavors.

Skilled marketers do the same thing before sitting down to craft a compelling message (or lay out an Intuitive Path). For them, in addition to knowing their ideal customer, there are four key elements that make up their marketing *mise-en-place*. Namely, they are the transformation, the motivation, the mechanism, and the proof:

THE TRANSFORMATION

As we explored previously, nobody buys anything unless there's something that they want but don't have, or something that they have but don't want. There's an "after picture" that is different from the "before picture" that they're living right now, which means that there's a transformation that takes them from "before" to "after." This may include very tangible and external transformations (what they have, what they do), and may also include very intangible and internal transformations (what they feel, what they are). Understanding that transformation is the first ingredient in the marketing *mise-en-place*.

THE MOTIVATION

Next comes motivation, which is an answer to the question of why they want the transformation in the first place. Now, the thing about motivation is that you can explore it on a very surface level or on a very deep level. We're looking to go as deep as we can here, to what professionals call *psychosocial motivations*. These come down to the different roles that we play in our lives, and a shortcut for getting at them is to fill in the blanks of this sentence:

As [ROLE], I should [OUTCOME].

The power of this fill-in-the-blanks exercise is that it gets at the deep ways in which your ideal customer feels that they aren't living up to who they are supposed to be. Consider these examples:

- As a parent, I should be able to keep my children safe.
- As a professional, I should be able to handle this sort of situation.
- As an educated member of society, I should be able to figure this out.

These examples illustrate the deep way in which your ideal customer might feel like they're falling short. Note, by the way, that you probably will never say these exact words to your ideal customer, as that would be far too "on the nose." The purpose of this exercise is to understand where they're coming from and what matters to them, so that we can speak to those needs and desires effectively later on.

THE MECHANISM

In 1966, Eugene Schwartz published *Breakthrough Advertising*, which has been called the "most important book written on persuasion, copywriting, marketing, and human behavior." Among the (many) good ideas put forth in the book, Schwartz explained the idea that markets go through predictable stages of increasing sophistication.

At the first stage, when a category of offer is brand-new, all you need is to state the benefit. The classic example is the diet pill industry (which, for the record, I'm not a fan of, but it does make for a good illustrative example). When the first diet pill came onto the market, all the marketers had to say was that taking this pill would help you lose weight. Since there had never been a pill that claimed to do that before, the bold claim was all that was needed.

But the success of any product will attract the attention of other opportunistic entrepreneurs. The entry of other players into the market brings us to the second stage, where benefits will be compared against each other by consumers. This requires quantification (e.g., "my pill will help you lose seven pounds in seven days" and then "eight pounds in six days" and so on).

Eventually we get to the third stage, which is where most markets continue to operate: There are lots of available options for consumers to choose from, and most consumers have already tried a solution (or several!) that hasn't worked. This means that consumers are skeptical that anything will work for them, and need to be given a reason to believe that your solution will work when others haven't. That reason is the mechanism that drives your offer: the "proprietary" or "patented" ingredient or the unique "system" or "formula" that only you possess.

THE PROOF

It's never been easier to make bombastic claims about what your product or service can do, and it's never been harder to get people to actually believe what you say, and for good reason; trust is famously at an all-time low, and whenever you make a claim, customers will instinctively wonder why they should believe you. The answer is proof; the more proof you can offer that your claims are true and you can deliver on them, the better. Proof can come in many forms, including:

- A compelling explanation
- A mechanism
- Endorsements from experts
- Case studies of customers
- A demonstration
- A creative guarantee

The more proof elements that you have available to layer into your offer, the better. And once you have your proof ready, along with your transformation, motivation, and mechanism, you'll be ready to mix them together into a story that connects the dots for your ideal customer, with what I call a Demand Narrative.

BRIDGE FROM NEED TO DESIRE

As an expert, you know what your audience needs, but it doesn't matter what *you* know. What matters is that they feel deeply enough to want to do something about it. You will create that feeling by constructing a Demand Narrative: the story that your audience will hear and experience that will bring them to the point of being ready to buy. It is the message that will take them from not knowing anything about your offer to having a burning desire for it. There are five steps to this process:

1. **DESCRIBE THEIR SYMPTOMS OR DESIRES ("THIS IS WHAT IT FEELS LIKE").** For any story to be compelling, the first step is to show relevance by meeting the audience where they are and speaking to the things that they care about. In practical terms, this means clearly and viscerally articulating either the symptoms of the pain they are currently experiencing, or the image in their head of the desired outcome that they want to move toward. There's no need for a deep root cause analysis of why they don't yet have the outcomes they want; that all comes later. The first step is to validate for the audience that they're in the right place and listening to the right person.

2. **ARTICULATE THEIR SELF-DIAGNOSIS ("IT'S NOT YOUR FAULT, BECAUSE...").** After validating that they're listening to the right person about the right topic, the second

step is to articulate their self-diagnosis of what's causing the problem, which will almost always include an externalization of responsibility (a.k.a. a reason why it's not their fault). Many of the coaches, consultants, speakers, authors, and experts that I work with find this step to be difficult and unintuitive, for the simple reason that the self-diagnosis is likely to be wrong (otherwise, they wouldn't need your help). As an expert, you know exactly what the problem really is, but you can't launch into that explanation yet. In order to earn the right and credibility to share what's really going on, you have to first show that you understand the world as they see it. This is done by articulating (and when possible validating) their understanding about what is standing in their way.

3. **SHARE THE DEEPER INSIGHT ("YOU THINK IT'S X, BUT REALLY IT'S Y").** Once you've shown that you understand what they're thinking and feeling, they'll be ready to hear what they're missing. This works only if you've laid the groundwork of the previous steps, but if you have, it is powerful. To paraphrase marketing legend Jay Abraham, if you can articulate the problem better than they can, they'll trust that you have a solution. This is where you share your deeper understanding of what's really causing their problem, which opens the door to a solution.

4. **EXPLAIN THE SOLUTION ("HERE'S HOW TO DO IT").** Having explained what really causes the problem, you can speak to the solution that can solve it. This will often tie in with the unique mechanism that we mentioned in the previous section.

5. **PROPOSE THE NEXT ACTION ("HERE'S YOUR NEXT STEP").** Finally, you're ready to invite them to whatever next step makes sense on the Intuitive Path that you're laying out.

Here are a few examples of what a very simple Demand Narrative might look like in a few different niches (the first two are fictional):

WEIGHT LOSS

- <u>Symptoms or Desires</u>: Do you keep trying to lose weight, but nothing you try seems to work?

- <u>Self-Diagnosis</u>: All the diet programs are bogus and impossible to stick with.

- <u>Deeper Insight</u>: You think it's about calories in versus calories out, but it's really about managing your metabolism.

- <u>Solution</u>: If you reset your metabolism, it will burn more calories all the time.

- <u>Next Action</u>: Explore our metabolism reset program.

PRODUCTIVITY

- <u>Symptoms or Desires</u>: Are you drowning in a sea of distraction, never getting to what matters?

- <u>Self-Diagnosis</u>: There's just too much to do, and there are too many demands on my time.

- <u>Deeper Insight</u>: It's not about time, it's about performance, and performance is most influenced by the quality of your sleep.

- <u>Solution</u>: If you improve the efficiency of your sleep, you'll be more productive every day.

- <u>Next Action</u>: Explore our sleep efficiency program.

MARKETING

- <u>Symptoms or Desires</u>: I never have enough customers, or enough dollars in the bank. I've tried everything, but none of the strategies that I've tried work the way the gurus say that they will.

- <u>Self-Diagnosis</u>: Marketing is hard, and requires specialized skills that I just don't have.

- <u>Deeper Insight</u>: Marketing is hard when your business is out of alignment with your customers.

- <u>Solution</u>: Create a more obvious offer, more resonant identity, and more intuitive path in your business.

- <u>Next Action</u>: Read my book *Effortless*.

The Demand Narrative is a powerful structure for bridging the gap from what you know your audience needs to what they truly desire. But desire isn't enough – for prospects to become customers, desire must translate to action.

Escalating Cycles of Commitment and Reward

"The early bird catches the worm."
"An ounce of prevention is worth a pound of cure."
"A stitch in time saves nine."
"One year's seeds, seven years of weeds."

These and many other common phrases remind us that in many areas of life, even more important than *what* we do is *when* we do it, and in what order. This is certainly true of the steps in the path that you lay out, if you want it to be truly intuitive. You probably have a laundry list of things that your prospect needs to know, understand, and believe before they will be ready to become your customer, but that doesn't mean you can just go through the list alphabetically and expect it to have the desired effect!

The steps need to be laid out in order of escalating engagement, so that you start with the smallest possible "ask," which leads to a small engagement, which gives you the opportunity to ask for a little more, which increases the engagement, and so forth. The goal, after all, is not just to convey knowledge. If it is well laid out, the Intuitive Path will engineer a shift in stance, from passive and skeptical prospect to actively engaged buyer.

So start with this: From where your prospect is sitting right now, what is an easy and reasonable request for you to make of them? Is it to watch a 30-second video? Read a web page? Take a quiz? Whatever it is, start with an enticing opportunity for them to get something interesting and valuable by making that small commitment. Then, when they take that step, overdeliver on the promised experience, showing them that it's more than worthwhile to make commitments and investments (of time, energy, attention, and eventually money) in their relationship with you. And then repeat the process, at each cycle pushing the boundary of the scale of investment that you invite them to make.

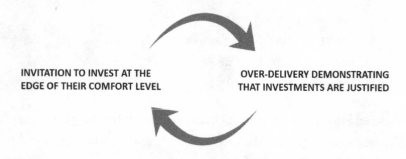

INVITATION TO INVEST AT THE
EDGE OF THEIR COMFORT LEVEL

OVER-DELIVERY DEMONSTRATING
THAT INVESTMENTS ARE JUSTIFIED

This underlying logic is why so many online marketing funnels that start with a small step like clicking on an ad or watching a short video escalate to small commitments like providing a name and email address, which leads to a more involved experience like an e-book or longer video, which leads to an invitation to a live training event like a webinar, which leads to an hour or more of training, which finally leads to a phone call and enrollment in a multi-thousand-dollar offer.

Where funnels often go wrong is that they copy this architecture of opportunities to make ever-deeper investments of time, energy, and attention (ad, then email capture, then video, etc.), but they forget to close the loop on each part of the cycle by overdelivering on the promises that were made. This defeats the purpose of this entire structure, or any other configuration that makes a path feel intuitive: At each stage the invitation should be small and easy to say "yes" to, because it is exactly the next step that they already want to take. And then they are rewarded for having taken that step. A well-designed Intuitive Path will incorporate as many of these cycles of commitment and reward as it takes to convey everything that the ideal customer needs to know, understand, and believe in order to be fully convinced of the truly irresistible nature of your offer.

WHAT'S INTUITIVE FOR B2B (OR COMPLEX BUYING CYCLES)?

Of the thousands upon thousands of coaches, consultants, speakers, authors, and experts whose business growth I've had the privilege of supporting, about a third operate in business-to-business (B2B) environments, meaning that they sell their programs and services into organizations. And while it's true that fundamentally every buyer is a person, there are differences in process and experience when you're selling to an organization with complex approval processes, multiple stakeholders to get on board, and specific budgetary criteria that need to be met.

But that's not to say that it can't be done, or even that it is particularly difficult. But it is *different*; what is intuitive in one context is completely unintuitive in another, which means that if you try to apply the same processes as you would in a business-to-consumer environment, it isn't likely to work very well. The key to navigating these differences is to understand the distinction between a buying *modality* and a buying *process*.

Buying modalities are primarily about the medium that moves someone from contemplation to action—for example, reading a sales letter, watching a sales presentation, or talking to a salesperson. The reason why online marketing can be so effective is that it is fairly easy to substitute one medium with another; for example, the printed sales letter can become a web page, the sales presentation can become a webinar or video, and the salesperson can work just as effectively over the phone or video conference, and can even be augmented by artificial intelligence through tools like Facebook Messenger bots.

Buying processes, on the other hand, are about the steps and stakeholders involved in reaching a sale—for example, the line manager, HR director, and VP of finance might all need to sign off on a sale, and it might have to go through two rounds of budgetary approval. Whereas there is a great deal of room to experiment with different buying modalities, the process itself is a lot harder to change, and attempts to circumvent the stakeholders and cycles are likely to end in failure. (Imagine telling a line manager that they don't need their bosses to be on board and that they have to skip the approval cycles, because the doors are closing tomorrow; that isn't likely to be effective!)

So if you're selling into a corporate environment (or any environment with a complex buying process), don't let the allure of automated internet marketing seduce you away from serving the people who need to be on board as they take the steps that they have to traverse. Remember that what we're ultimately solving for is an Intuitive Path, and a path can only be intuitive in the eyes of the ideal customers that you are looking to serve.

Case Study: The Path to LIFT

I'll illustrate the ideas in this chapter by sharing the Intuitive Path that we've laid out, leading the right people to go from skeptical strangers to engaged customers. Our ideal customer, if you recall, is a coach, consultant, speaker, author, or expert who is looking to grow their leverage, freedom, and impact through the vehicle of an online business. Before they are ready to invest in our training or coaching programs, there are things that they need to know, understand, and believe about the opportunity, about themselves, and about our offer:

- **ABOUT THE OPPORTUNITY –** That it is possible to create leverage, freedom, and impact by building an expertise-driven business, through some combination of coaching, consulting, online courses, and other offerings, both offline and online.

- **ABOUT THEMSELVES –** That their expertise is valuable enough to capitalize on the opportunity to build that sort of business, and that they have the capacity and fortitude to learn and do what will be needed to make that happen.

- **ABOUT THE OFFER –** That my team and I know what it takes to seize that opportunity, have the skills and resources to lead and support their journey to making it happen, and that we can be trusted to deliver on our promises and put our students' interests first.

My *mise-en-place* of marketing ingredients, which will come into play as we develop a marketing message and path, includes the following transformation, motivation, mechanism, and proof:

- **TRANSFORMATION** – The transformation that our customers seek is about going from a "before picture" of not having a thriving expertise-driven business to the "after picture" of having one. Externally, that means the tangible trappings of leverage, freedom, and impact: making the money that they want to make without spending more time than they feel is reasonable, investing their time and resources in the places and people that they care about most, and seeing the world become better for their efforts. Internally, that transformation often involves going from a place of uncertainty, insecurity, and anxiety to a place of confidence, clarity, and competence.

- **MOTIVATION** – A deeper look at the motivation driving our customers reveals the feeling that they aren't making full use of the gifts that they've been given. It's the feeling that they're meant for more and that they aren't currently living up to their full potential.

- **MECHANISM** – Our audience is likely to have seen other companies and personalities promising that they can "teach you to get rich on the internet" and have likely been turned off by their style and message, burned by their experience, or both. That's why we need a very strong answer when they ask us how we can give them hope that we can help them when others haven't, and while there are a lot of proof elements that we can point to (see below), at the core, what we offer is a different perspective on how expertise-based businesses are successfully built (the framework and methodology that you're reading about in this book).

- **PROOF** – Without proof, everything is just an empty promise. That's why we back up our promises with all the proof that we can muster, including the case studies of thousands of businesses we've helped, the messages of experts who have endorsed our work, and the strongest guarantee in our industry (our ACES program guarantees that you will make back 100% of your investment and break the bottlenecks that are holding back your growth; otherwise, we will keep working with you until you do). This book is a proof element, too, in that you're getting to know about our process, which hopefully makes intuitive sense to you as you read it. And you're getting to know me and the way I think, which hopefully resonates with you (if you're my ideal customer, that is).

These "ingredients" mix together to create the following high-level Demand Narrative, which we can then map onto specific steps in an Intuitive Path:

Symptoms or Desires: Not enough leads, therefore not enough customers, therefore not enough revenue. This creates stress and frustration, because options are limited and everything feels precarious, and all the while your potential for impact is being hidden away from the world.

<u>Self-Diagnosis</u>: I'm good at my area of expertise, but not good at the business (or online marketing) side of it all. And I don't know if I even want to be good at that part; I want to focus on doing my good work, rather than getting good at marketing that makes me uncomfortable.

<u>Deeper Insight</u>: Rather than getting better at selling, why not focus on making it easier for people to buy? Instead of pushing harder, you can work to remove the friction that will get in their way of taking action with you.

<u>Solution</u>: The Effortless Business Growth model, which codifies how to design your Obvious Offer, cultivate your Resonant Identity, and lay out your Intuitive Path.

<u>Next Action</u>: Join our ACES Business Acceleration Program and we'll help you create that effortless growth in your business.

Now, so far this is all background and messaging points—so what does it look like in practice? There's a lot to convey here, and a lot to cover. So we do it incrementally, starting with high-quality information that is cheap or free (like this book and the associated training, and also many other resources that can be found on our website). Once we're in relationship with a prospect (meaning that we have their name and email address), we send targeted and helpful materials meant to support their growth, and drive home the various points that are important for us to make. Note that it is important that the materials we send actually be helpful, because much of what must be conveyed has to be shown rather than told; if I want you to believe I am trustworthy, it works a lot better to do things that are legitimately helpful and in your best interest than to just say "trust me!"

Eventually, when people are ready, we invite them to attend our three-day LIFT training experience, where we cover such topics as phases of business growth, entrepreneurial decision-making, marketing, and creating great online courses, and everything in between. The event is designed to catalyze and accelerate the growth of our customers' businesses, and for those who are ready, a gentle invitation to join the ACES program is extended. It doesn't need to be more than that gentle invitation, because for those who are a good fit, much of what they need to know, understand, and believe has already been internalized through their firsthand experience with us.

Chapter Review

Wondering whether you caught every idea in this chapter? Or just looking to review? Here's a quick summary of the ideas that we covered here:

- Before getting to a place where they're ready to invest a substantial amount of time, money, and energy in anything, there are things that your future customer needs to know, understand, and believe—about the broader opportunity in which you operate, about themselves, and of course about you and your offer.
    - About the opportunity: They need to believe that the problem that they're looking to solve is actually solvable.
    - About themselves: Everyone feels like they are a unique, special snowflake, and it's not enough that a solution can work for some people—it has to feel workable to them.
    - About you and your offer: They have to understand the relevancy of your offer to their needs ("why this?"), your credibility to deliver ("why you?"), and the urgency to act on a solution ("why now?").

- All of these things must be communicated to your ideal prospect before they will be ready to become your ideal customer.

- Before you begin laying out your path, you must gather your ingredients: the transformation (from "before picture" to "after picture"), the motivation (completing the sentence "As [ROLE], I should [OUTCOME]."), the mechanism (to give them hope that your solution will work where others haven't), and the proof (that you can deliver on your promises).

- The bridge from need to desire follows a straightforward and predictable path:
    - Describe Their Symptoms or Desires ("this is what it feels like").
    - Articulate Their Self-Diagnosis ("it's not your fault, because...").
    - Share the Deeper Insight ("you think it's X, but really it's Y").
    - Explain the Solution ("here's how to do it").
    - Propose the Next Action ("here's your next step").

As you take people through this narrative, you must also bring them through escalating cycles of commitment and reward, at each turn inviting them to make a slightly larger investment of time, energy, attention, or money—and then rewarding them for having done so!

This process applies to B2B customers just as it does to B2C, but the specifics of how you will render the process into a marketing path will look different, based on what is intuitive to their expectations and processes.

Additional resources to support you!

GET THE AUDIOBOOK + EFFORTLESS BUSINESS GROWTH TOOLKIT

Get the free audiobook PLUS our Effortless Business Growth Toolkit, which contains valuable downloads and worksheets to help you apply these concepts to your business.

→ Download it at **Effortless.Rocks/toolkit**

ATTEND A FREE EFFORTLESS BUSINESS GROWTH WORKSHOP

Ready to lay out an Intuitive Path that leads to effortless growth in your business? Attend our free online workshop to go deeper into the ideas in this book, and put them into practice.

→ Sign up for free at **Effortless.Rocks/workshop**

JOIN US IN PERSON AT LIFT

Discover cutting-edge strategies to accelerate your business growth through our immersive 3-day training experience for coaches, consultants, authors, speakers, and expert entrepreneurs.

→ Reserve your spot at **Effortless.Rocks/lift**

CHAPTER 5
The Opposite of Futility

> *"Rome wasn't built in a day,*
> *but they were laying bricks every hour."*
> —James Clear

IMAGINE A PLANK being held in place by two sets of springs, one set on each side. If you want to move the plank in one direction, you could either add springs on one side, or remove springs on the other. Either way will work, but if you add springs there will be a lot more tension applied to the plank. On the other hand, if you remove springs, the overall tension decreases.

This thought experiment was described by economics Nobel laureate and author of the modern behavior economics classic *Thinking, Fast and Slow*, Daniel Kahneman, in an interview on Shane Parrish's *The Knowledge Project* podcast. It is the perfect illustration of the philosophy for business growth that I've laid out in this book. You can always push harder, but it's better and easier to engineer a more obvious offer, a more resonant identity, and a more intuitive path to make the process of business growth increasingly more effortless.

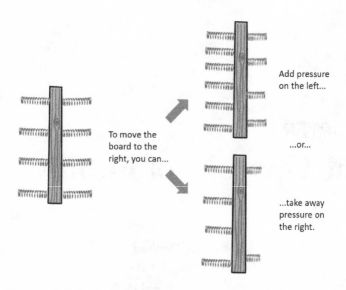

To move the board to the right, you can...

Add pressure on the left...

...or...

...take away pressure on the right.

That's the core of a good strategy: building a sustainable advantage that gets stronger and stronger over time. But the thing about creating Effortless Business Growth is that when you're just starting, it will take a fair amount of effort!

Effort Leading to Effortlessness

Our last in-person LIFT event, before the COVID-19 pandemic forced everything to go virtual, was held in my hometown of Montreal in August 2019. One of the excellent guest speakers that shared ideas and strategies with our audience was Dorie Clark, the author of books like *Reinventing You*, *Stand Out*, and *Entrepreneurial You*, whom you met earlier in this book. From the stage she told the story of her mother's choice as an adult to get braces for her teeth. Friends asked if it would be uncomfortable? Inconvenient? A huge hassle? Sure, replied Clark's mother. But a year from now I can be a year older, or a year older with straight teeth.

The message, of course, is that the time will pass anyway, so you might as well spend it doing the stuff that will improve things once the time has passed. It's a wise message, and it applies very well to the ideas presented in this book. In addition to sharing the specifics of identifying your ideal customer and creating your Obvious Offer, Resonant Identity, and Intuitive Path, I've also not-so-subtly suggested that while the outcome of this process is Effortless Business Growth, the process of creating it does in fact require a fair amount of well-directed effort.

This is similar in concept to business writer Jim Collins's ideas around building a flywheel. The first few turns on that flywheel are likely to be laborious and difficult, because there is no momentum to build on. But with every effortful turn on that flywheel, it picks up a bit more speed, and the energy required to keep it spinning and accelerating declines. The same dynamic applies to the creation of Effortless Business Growth. And that dynamic can feel daunting—there's so much to do, and none of it feels easy. So where should you begin?

There is a "right" way to choose what comes first, second, and third: analyzing your business to find the current bottleneck that is throttling your growth, and focusing your efforts there. Eventually, you will have broken the constraint, and the bottleneck will move to somewhere else in your business. In this way, you might jump from making your path more intuitive, to making your identity more resonant, to making your offer more obvious, and around again. The order will change, and the cycle will never end. The results, however, will keep getting better.

That said, what matters a lot more than starting at the "right" place is just starting (if you're not sure where, just work the levers in the same order that they appear in this book: offer, then identity, then path). To paraphrase General George Patton, rapid and strong execution of a less-than-perfect plan is much better than sitting on your hands as you slowly search for the best place to start. The most important thing is that you do something—anything!—to make your offer more obvious, your identity more resonant, and your path more intuitive. The more steps you take, the more Effortless things will become.

It will be nearly imperceptible at first, but the improvements will have a compounding effect—getting 1% better each week doesn't feel like much, but within a couple of years it adds up to a dramatic improvement in the effectiveness of your business. The early steps aren't easy, but they're worth it for the path that they put you on. And you might as well get started; a year from now, you'll be a year older either way, so you might as well be a year older with an effortlessly growing business.

Never Finished

The more obvious your offer, resonant your identity, and intuitive your path, the more effortless it will be for your business to grow and thrive, but that doesn't mean you can rest on your laurels. Early in this book, I told you about the ice cream options in my neighborhood, with the local-owned, artisanal, good-but-not-perfect Sandrini coming out on top. But nothing stands still; since writing those words, two major disruptions came on the scene. The first was dramatic: the COVID-19 pandemic, which changed just about everything for everyone. The ice cream shops all did a pretty good job of adapting to take-out operations. But then, after successfully adapting to the disruption of COVID-19, Sandrini faced a more mundane challenge. Just a couple of months before penning this last chapter, a new contender entered the fray: Café Gelato. It's the same distance to my house as Sandrini, but in the other direction. They are local-owned and serve delicious artisanal gelato and vegan sorbets. Unlike Sandrini, they have a generous amount of seating space, and the lines move a lot faster. Much as I'd like to describe myself as a loyal customer who supports local businesses, my family and I haven't been back to Sandrini since Café Gelato opened. Their offer is just more obvious to us.

It's true that the more you lean into your Obvious Offer, Resonant Identity, and Intuitive Path, the easier things will get. But that doesn't mean you can take your foot off the pedal or your eye off the ball, because the world of business is dynamic and constantly changing. Competitors enter the scene, customer needs and wants evolve, and every so often the entire landscape of business is hit by an asteroid-scale disruption, like COVID-19. So enjoy the increasing effortlessness, but keep on pushing yourself to make your Offer even more Obvious, your Identity even more Resonant, and your Path even more Intuitive. And stay attuned to your ideal customer and what they truly want and need... not a month or a year or a decade ago, but now, and into the future. Leonardo da Vinci famously said that "art is never finished, only abandoned"—the same is true for Effortless Business Growth.

What is always true about growth that is effortless is that effortlessness goes both ways. Throughout this book we've explored what it takes to make the growth of your business effortless, because that's what you (the business owner) care about. But what we've also been talking about is making the experience of working with you effortless for your customers. That's the real key. The more effortless it is for them, the more effortless it will be for you.

Additional resources to support you!

GET THE AUDIOBOOK + EFFORTLESS BUSINESS GROWTH TOOLKIT

Get the free audiobook PLUS our Effortless Business Growth Toolkit, which contains valuable downloads and worksheets to help you apply these concepts to your business.

→ Download it at **Effortless.Rocks/toolkit**

ATTEND A FREE EFFORTLESS BUSINESS GROWTH WORKSHOP

Ready to lay out an Intuitive Path that leads to effortless growth in your business? Attend our free online workshop to go deeper into the ideas in this book, and put them into practice.

→ Sign up for free at **Effortless.Rocks/workshop**

JOIN US IN PERSON AT LIFT

Discover cutting-edge strategies to accelerate your business growth through our immersive 3-day training experience for coaches, consultants, authors, speakers, and expert entrepreneurs.

→ Reserve your spot at **Effortless.Rocks/lift**

Download the AudioBook + Effortless Business Course Toolkit (for FREE)!

READ THIS FIRST

Just to say thank you for reading my book, I'd love to share the audiobook version PLUS our accompanying Effortless Business Growth Toolkit, at no cost whatsoever – it's my gift to you.

— Danny Iny

Go to **www.Effortless.Rocks/toolkit** to get it!

In the Agency of Others

"Greatness is in the agency of others."
—Scott Galloway

THE MORE BOOKS I WRITE, the more I come to appreciate that book writing is a team sport. Without many, many great people around me, I wouldn't have the knowledge or experience about which to write, the time or focus to put proverbial pen to paper, or even the logistical support to turn my typo-riddled manuscript into the near-pristine work that you hold in your hand.

Topping the list are the wonderful people that I get to work with every day at Mirasee, where we teach coaches, consultants, authors, speakers and experts to teach their gift and grow their businesses—and of course the students that we have the privilege of working with, supporting, and also learning from.

Special thanks go to Joey Gourdji and the entire team involved in the creation of our three-day LIFT training experience, where many of these ideas about Effortless Business Growth were first shared and pilot-tested.

Deep gratitude also to Ally Machate and the entire publishing team behind her at The Writer's Ally. Thank you for making the book in my hands better than I imagined it would be in my mind.

And most of all, my family. Bhoomi, you are my partner at home, and my partner at work. I hit the marriage jackpot, and tempted as I sometimes am to take that for granted, I will do my best to always remember how lucky I am. Priya and Micah, I'm so proud of you both—your poise, your curiosity, your initiative, and everything else that makes you both so wonderful. It is my privilege to watch you grow and to learn so much from you both.

About the Author

DANNY INY is the founder and CEO of the online business education company Mirasee, whose work on strategy training won special recognition from *Fast Company* as a "World Changing Idea." He has been featured in the *Harvard Business Review* and *Entrepreneur*, and contributes regularly to publications including *Inc., Forbes*, and *Business Insider*. He has spoken at institutions like Yale University and organizations like Google, and is the author of multiple books about online courses and education, including two editions of *Teach and Grow Rich* (in 2015 and 2017), *Leveraged Learning* (in 2018) and *Teach Your Gift* (in 2020). He lives in Montreal, Canada, with his wife Bhoomi (who is his partner in both life and business) and their children Priya and Micah.

CPSIA information can be obtained
at www.ICGtesting.com
Printed in the USA
BVHW050557240322
632050BV00003B/9